LOW-FAT
WAYS TO COOK FOR
THE HOLIDAYS

D1497513

LOW-FAT
WAYS TO COOK FOR
THE HOLIDAYS

COMPILED AND EDITED BY
SUSAN M. MCINTOSH, M.S., R.D.

Oxmoor
House®

Library of Congress Catalog Number: 98-67025
ISBN: 0-8487-2217-5
Manufactured in the United States of America
First Printing 1998

Editor-in-Chief: Nancy Fitzpatrick Wyatt
Editorial Director, Special Interest Publications: Ann H. Harvey
Senior Foods Editor: Katherine M. Eakin
Senior Editor, Editorial Services: Olivia Kindig Wells
Art Director: James Boone

LOW-FAT WAYS TO COOK FOR THE HOLIDAYS

Menu and Recipe Consultant: Susan McEwen McIntosh, M.S., R.D.
Assistant Editor: Kelly Hooper Troiano
Associate Foods Editor: Anne Chappell Cain, M.S., M.P.H., R.D.
Copy Editor: Keri Bradford Anderson
Editorial Assistants: Robin Boteler, Suzanne Powell
Indexer: Mary Ann Laurens
Associate Art Director: Cynthia R. Cooper
Designer: Carol Damsky
Senior Photographer: Jim Bathie
Photographers: Howard L. Puckett, Becky Luigart-Stayner,
   Cooking Light magazine; Ralph Anderson, Brit Huckabay;
   Barbara Bordnick (page 43); Louis Wallach (pages 74, 75);
   élan Modeling Agency, Birmingham, Alabama (page 131)
Senior Photo Stylist: Kay E. Clarke
Photo Stylists: Cindy Manning Barr, Cathy Muir, *Cooking Light* magazine;
   Virginia R. Cravens
Director, Production and Distribution: Phillip Lee
Associate Production Manager: Vanessa Cobbs Richardson
Production Assistant: Faye Porter Bonner

Our appreciation to the staff of *Cooking Light* magazine and to the Southern
Progress Corporation library staff for their contributions to this book.

Cover: *Fudgy Mint Brownie Dessert (recipe on page 115), Frosted Sugar Cookies
   (recipe on page 132), Linzer Cookies (recipe on page 136)*
Frontispiece: *Cranberry Conserve and Pear and Apple Chutney (recipes on page 125)*

We're Here for You!

We at Oxmoor House are
dedicated to serving you with
reliable information that expands
your imagination and enriches your
life. We welcome your comments
and suggestions. Please write us at:

Oxmoor House, Inc.
Editor, *Low-Fat Ways To Cook
   for the Holidays*
2100 Lakeshore Drive
Birmingham, AL 35209

CONTENTS

CELEBRATE WITH EASE! 6

HOLIDAY MENUS 11

FAMILY THANKSGIVING DINNER 12
CELEBRATION OF LIGHTS 15
FESTIVE DINNER PARTY 19
WELCOME CHRISTMAS MORNING 21
EASY HOLIDAY BRUNCH 24
NEW YEAR'S EVE GALA 27
HAPPY NEW YEAR BUFFET 32

FESTIVE BEGINNINGS 37

FROM THE BREAD BASKET 51

ELEGANT ENTRÉES 69

SIDE-DISH FAVORITES 85

CLASSIC DESSERTS 99

TREATS FROM THE KITCHEN 121

INDEX 141
METRIC EQUIVALENTS 144

CELEBRATE WITH EASE!

The holiday season is a time of friendly get-togethers, office parties, open houses, and traditional family dinners, all of which center around wonderful food. Now, with the recipes in this book, you can cut back the fat while keeping traditions alive. And the suggestions below will help you do it all with ease, leaving you with enough energy to enjoy the festivities.

If you are like most people, you have little time during the busy period from Thanksgiving to New Year's Day to prepare complicated recipes. But you *can* serve traditional holiday foods—just plan realistic menus and schedule your time wisely. The following pages show you how to do this so that your holiday meals—and gift-giving—go smoothly.

Take the guesswork out of holiday meal planning— turn to page 24 for this low-fat menu designed for a celebration.

PLANNING AHEAD

During the holidays, meal planning, preparation, and serving become more complicated than usual. But don't panic. If you organize early, you can dazzle your family and friends with delicious recipes and still be cool and confident enough to have fun. Whether you are expecting a large number of guests for an open-house buffet or just a few friends for a sit-down dinner, you can remain calm by following these tips.

• **Plan a menu** that will appeal to most of your guests. Pick recipes that provide a variety of colors, tastes, textures, and temperatures.

• **Write down your menu** and be sure to indicate where to find the recipes. (Try the section on holiday menus beginning on page 11 for suggestions that you can adapt to your own needs.)

• **Limit the number of dishes** that require last-minute cooking. The more you can do ahead of time, the better. Don't make every dish complicated, or you'll end up frustrated. Coordinate recipes so that you won't have to bake more dishes at the last minute than your oven can hold.

• **Pick make-ahead recipes.** Prepare cakes, pies, cookies, breads, and casseroles that you can make in advance and then refrigerate or freeze until needed. You can usually make salad dressings, gelatin salads, and chilled desserts one or two days ahead. Sauces, pickles, and relishes, all of which can be made ahead, add distinction to an otherwise simple meal.

Prepare Fluffy Fruit Dip with Almond Chips (page 31) up to two days ahead of time. On party day, wash and slice the fruit.

• **Make two grocery lists.** The first should include items that you can buy and store or use in recipes prepared ahead of time. The second list should be for perishables that have to be purchased a day or two before the party.

For large gatherings, you will want to take a few other organizational steps.

• **Write out three time schedules.** The first schedule should include anything you can do several days ahead, such as preparing make-ahead recipes, checking linens, polishing silver, and ordering items that must be rented. The second schedule should organize all preparation that will need to be done the day of the party. Allow extra time to relax and to get ready in time to greet early arrivals. A third schedule should detail everything you have to do while guests are in your home. Keep a list on the counter that indicates what to do, right down to when to preheat the oven and how long to bake the bread.

• **Gather cookware** and serving dishes. Make sure you won't need more baking pans than you own or can borrow.

• **Pull out serving utensils**, platters, and bowls for every dish on the menu; label how you'll use them.

GIFTS FROM THE KITCHEN

Prepare jars of Cranberry Jezebel Sauce (page 124) to give throughout the holidays.

Holiday gift buying is often as challenging as menu planning. Make it easier on yourself *and*

delight your friends by stirring up homemade food gifts a few days or even weeks ahead of time. You'll find several delicious, low-fat choices in the final chapter of this book. They include such specialties as Cranberry Jezebel Sauce, Curried Peppercorn Mustard (page 123), and Apple Butter (page 124), each of which can be made and then stored in the refrigerator up to three weeks.

You can also prepare recipes such as Peppered Cheese Chips (page 123) and Italian Seasoned Snack Mix (page 124) to store in airtight containers at room temperature. Set aside some space in your freezer for food gifts of Apple Spice Minicakes (page 140) and some of the cookies featured on pages 126 through 139.

FACTS ON FREEZING

Freezing foods for the holidays is easy when you know a few basics. Learn which foods freeze well, how long they keep, and how to package and store them correctly.

• Many baked goods, meats, poultry, casseroles, soups, and stews freeze well. Avoid freezing dishes that contain mayonnaise (it separates when frozen), salad greens (they become limp), and cooked egg whites (they become tough). Cook dishes containing raw rice before you freeze them.

• Use moisture-proof, airtight, and odorless packaging, such as zip-top plastic freezer bags, plastic-coated freezer paper, rigid freezer-safe plastic or glass containers with tight fitting lids, heavy-duty aluminum foil, and heavy-duty plastic wrap. Do not use plastic sandwich or storage bags, produce bags, bread bags, or plastic tubs. Pack food tightly to eliminate as much air as possible, and tightly seal all containers, bags, and other packaging.

To freeze a casserole, line with heavy-duty aluminum foil, leaving a generous overhang; add food. Freeze until firm. Remove foil and frozen food. Fold overhang to seal; label and return to freezer. Then you can use the dish for other purposes.

• Make sure the temperature in your freezer is 0°F or lower. If the temperature is higher than that, food quality may suffer.

• For best quality, freeze foods soon after making them. Chill cooked foods in the refrigerator before placing them in the freezer so they will freeze faster. All you have to do with baked goods such as breads, cakes, and cookies is cool them to room temperature before freezing. Allow room for air to circulate around the food while it freezes; once it's frozen, stack the food closely.

• Label and date all food you freeze for easy identification. Keep a list of the freezer's contents. Also write down last-minute details such as cooking directions, baking time, baking temperature, number of servings, and recommended garnishes.

• Frozen baked goods such as cookies, cakes, breads, and pies remain at optimum quality up to one month. Casseroles, meatballs, meat loaves, and soups are best used within a month. You can freeze large cuts of meat or poultry up to three months. To prevent spoilage and retain quality, thaw frozen foods in the refrigerator before reheating.

From Freezer to Table

• The safest way to defrost frozen food is to transfer it to the refrigerator about eight hours before you plan to serve it. Do not let dishes that contain meat, fish, eggs, or poultry defrost at room temperature.

• You can reheat frozen soups, sauces, and stews on the cooktop without defrosting. Cook over low heat to prevent scorching, adding just enough water to cover the pan's bottom, or use a double boiler. Stir often to break up the food.

• Frozen casseroles reheat faster if defrosted. If you don't have time to defrost, cover with foil and bake in a moderate oven. Use bubbling edges and brownness as guides to timing.

• To reheat in the microwave oven, follow the directions in the owner's manual. Defrost large quantities of food at LOW (30% power) before reheating. Stir large quantities every 2 minutes; avoid overcooking. You don't need to defrost small quantities of food, but you should stir them often.

LOW-FAT BASICS

*W*hether you are trying to lose or maintain weight, low-fat eating makes good sense. Research studies show that decreasing your fat intake reduces risks of heart disease, diabetes, and some types of cancer. The goal recommended by major health groups is an intake of 30 percent or less of total daily calories.

The *Low-Fat Ways To Cook* series gives you practical, delicious recipes with realistic advice about low-fat cooking and eating. The recipes are lower in total fat than traditional recipes. In fact, most provide less than 30 percent from fat and less than 10 percent from saturated fat.

If you have one high-fat item during a meal, you can balance it with low-fat choices for the rest of the day and still remain within the recommended percentage. For example, fat contributes 42 percent of the calories in the broccoli side dish for the Thanksgiving dinner menu beginning on page 12. However, because the broccoli is served with other low-fat foods, the total menu provides only 16 percent of calories as fat.

The goal of fat reduction is not to eliminate fat entirely. In fact, a small amount of fat is needed to transport fat-soluble vitamins and maintain other normal body functions.

FIGURING THE FAT

The easiest way to achieve a diet with 30 percent or fewer of total calories from fat is to establish a daily "fat budget" based on the total number of calories you need each day. Multiply your current weight by 15 to estimate your daily calorie requirements. Remember that calorie requirements vary according to age, body size, and level of activity. To gain or lose 1 pound a week, add or subtract 500 calories a day. (A diet of fewer than 1,200 calories is not recommended unless medically supervised.)

To calculate your recommended fat allowance, multiply your daily calorie needs by .30 and divide by 9 (the number of calories in each gram of fat). You daily fat gram intake should not exceed this number. For quick reference, see the Daily Fat Limits chart.

DAILY FAT LIMITS		
Calories Per Day	30 Percent of Calories	Grams of Fat
1,200	360	40
1,500	450	50
1,800	540	60
2,000	600	67
2,200	660	73
2,500	750	83
2,800	840	93

NUTRITIONAL ANALYSIS

Each recipe in *Low-Fat Ways To Cook for the Holidays* has been kitchen-tested by a staff of food professionals. In addition, registered dietitians have determined the nutrient information using a computer system that analyzes every ingredient. These efforts ensure the success of the recipes and will help you fit them into your own meal planning.

The nutrient grid that follows each recipe provides calories per serving and the percentage of calories from fat. The grid also lists the grams of total fat, saturated fat, protein, and carbohydrate, and the milligrams of cholesterol and sodium per serving. The nutrient values are as accurate as possible and are based on the following assumptions:

• When a range is given for an ingredient (3 to 3½ cups, for instance), the lesser amount is calculated.

• When a recipe calls for cooked pasta or rice, we base the analysis on cooking without salt or fat.

• The calculations indicate that meat and poultry are trimmed of fat and skin before cooking.

• Only the amount of marinade absorbed by the food is calculated.

• When a recipe calls for "margarine," the analysis is based on regular stick margarine. If "reduced-calorie margarine" is specified, the analysis is based on reduced-calorie stick margarine.

• Garnishes and other optional ingredients are not calculated.

• Recipes calling for eggs or egg whites were tested with and analyzed for large eggs or egg whites.

• Fruit and vegetables are unpeeled unless specified.

Herb-Roasted Turkey (recipe on page 12)

HOLIDAY MENUS

Thanksgiving Day and turkey. Hanukkah and potato pancakes. New Year's Day and black-eyed peas. Some holiday food traditions should never be broken, even when menus are lightened. And with the healthful, creative recipes in this chapter, you can serve long-time favorites, cut fat and calories, *and* keep all the great taste.

These pages offer a delicious Thanksgiving dinner complete with Herb-Roasted Turkey (page 12) and Cranberry-Glazed Sweet Potatoes (page 14). You'll also find a Hanukkah menu featuring Mandelbrot (page 17) in the shape of the Star of David; a Christmas brunch to welcome family and guests; and a New Year's Eve buffet that offers festive fare like Holiday Glögg (page 27) and Curried Mushroom Turnovers (page 30). Every menu gives you practical tips on meal preparation along with photographs that suggest garnishes and serving ideas.

FAMILY THANKSGIVING DINNER
(pictured on page 10)

Begin the holiday season with this elegant, easy-to-prepare menu. Get a head start by preparing and freezing the soufflés up to two weeks ahead. If you purchase a frozen turkey, remember to transfer it to the refrigerator three to four days early to allow it to thaw completely by the time you start roasting it on Thanksgiving morning.

Herb-Roasted Turkey

Broccoli with Roasted Peppers

Barley, Wild Rice, and Currant Pilaf

Cranberry-Glazed Sweet Potatoes

French Silk Soufflés

Serves 8
TOTAL CALORIES PER SERVING: 751
(CALORIES FROM FAT: 16%)

HERB-ROASTED TURKEY

1 (12-pound) turkey
8 fresh thyme sprigs, divided
6 fresh rosemary sprigs, divided
6 fresh sage sprigs, divided
½ teaspoon poultry seasoning
¼ teaspoon salt
¼ teaspoon pepper
1 medium onion, quartered
2 stalks celery, each cut into 4 pieces
Vegetable cooking spray
Additional fresh rosemary, sage, and thyme
    sprigs (optional)
Orange wedges (optional)
Green and red grapes (optional)

Remove and discard giblets and neck from turkey. Rinse turkey under cold running water; pat dry. Trim excess fat. Starting at neck cavity, loosen skin from breast and drumsticks by inserting one hand, palm side down. Gently push hand beneath the skin against the meat to loosen.

Arrange a thyme sprig beneath skin on each drumstick. Arrange 2 sprigs each of thyme, rosemary, and sage beneath skin on each breast half. Gently press skin to secure.

Combine poultry seasoning, salt, and pepper. Sprinkle body cavity with half of seasoning mixture. Place 2 onion quarters, 4 celery pieces, and 1 sprig each of thyme, rosemary, and sage into body cavity. Repeat procedure for neck cavity.

If excess skin around tail has been cut away, tuck legs under flap of skin around tail. If excess skin is intact, close body cavity with skewers, and truss. Tie ends of legs to tail with cord. Lift wing tips up and over back, and tuck under turkey.

Place turkey, breast side up, on a rack coated with cooking spray; place rack in a shallow roasting pan. Coat turkey with cooking spray. Insert meat thermometer into meaty part of thigh, making sure it does not touch bone. Cover loosely with aluminum foil; bake at 325° for 2 hours. Uncover; bake 1 hour. Cut cord holding the drumstick ends to the tail (to ensure that thighs cook internally). Bake, uncovered, 30 additional minutes or until meat thermometer registers 180°. Cover turkey loosely with aluminum foil; let stand 20 minutes. Place on a serving platter; if desired, garnish with fresh herbs, oranges, and grapes. Yield: 23 servings.

PER SERVING: 144 CALORIES (26% FROM FAT)
FAT 4.1G (SATURATED FAT 1.4G)
PROTEIN 24.9G CARBOHYDRATE 0.0G
CHOLESTEROL 64MG SODIUM 85MG

BROCCOLI WITH ROASTED PEPPERS

3 large sweet red peppers
3 tablespoons lemon juice
1 tablespoon olive oil
¼ teaspoon salt
¼ teaspoon pepper
2 cloves garlic, minced
8 cups fresh broccoli flowerets
¼ cup sliced ripe olives

Cut red peppers in half lengthwise; discard seeds and membranes. Place peppers, skin sides up, on a baking sheet; flatten with palm of hand. Broil 5½ inches from heat (with electric oven door partially opened) 10 minutes or until blackened. Place peppers in zip-top plastic bag; seal and let stand 15 minutes. Peel and cut into 2- x ¼-inch strips. Combine pepper strips, lemon juice, and next 4 ingredients; toss well. Cover and chill.

Arrange broccoli in a steamer basket; cover and steam 4 minutes or until crisp-tender. Drain and rinse with cold water; drain well. Combine broccoli and olives in a bowl; toss gently. Cover and chill. Add red pepper mixture to broccoli mixture; toss gently. Yield: 8 (1-cup) servings.

Note: Substitute 2 (7-ounce) jars roasted sweet red peppers, drained, for 3 large sweet red peppers, if desired. (Omit procedure for roasting peppers.)

PER SERVING: 56 CALORIES (42% FROM FAT)
FAT 2.6G (SATURATED FAT 0.4G)
PROTEIN 3.0G CARBOHYDRATE 7.6G
CHOLESTEROL 0MG SODIUM 135MG

BARLEY, WILD RICE, AND CURRANT PILAF

½ cup pearl barley, uncooked
¼ cup wild rice, uncooked
1 teaspoon vegetable oil
¾ cup finely chopped onion
⅔ cup finely chopped celery
½ cup finely chopped carrot
1 clove garlic, minced
⅓ cup currants
1 teaspoon rubbed sage
½ teaspoon salt
½ teaspoon dried thyme
¼ teaspoon pepper
2 (10½-ounce) cans low-sodium chicken broth
1 bay leaf

Place barley and rice in a large skillet over medium heat. Cook 7 minutes or until lightly browned, stirring often. Place in a bowl; set aside.

Heat oil in skillet until hot. Add onion and next 3 ingredients; stir well. Cover and cook over medium-low heat 8 minutes or until vegetables are tender, stirring occasionally.

Add barley mixture, currants, and remaining ingredients to skillet; bring to a boil. Cover, reduce heat, and simmer mixture 50 minutes or until liquid is absorbed, stirring occasionally. Remove and discard bay leaf. Yield: 8 (½-cup) servings.

PER SERVING: 105 CALORIES (13% FROM FAT)
FAT 1.5G (SATURATED FAT 0.2G)
PROTEIN 3.3G CARBOHYDRATE 21.0G
CHOLESTEROL 0MG SODIUM 187MG

CRANBERRY-GLAZED SWEET POTATOES

6 medium-size sweet potatoes, peeled and cut
    into 1-inch pieces (about 3 pounds)
½ cup firmly packed brown sugar
2 tablespoons stick margarine
2 tablespoons unsweetened orange juice
½ teaspoon salt
1 cup whole-berry cranberry sauce
Orange rind (optional)

Place potato in a 2-quart microwave-safe baking
dish; cover and microwave at HIGH 12 minutes or
until potato is tender.

Combine sugar and next 3 ingredients in a 2-cup
glass measuring cup. Microwave at HIGH 3 minutes, stirring every minute. Add sugar mixture and
cranberry sauce to potato; toss gently. Microwave at
HIGH 10 minutes or until thoroughly heated, basting with sauce twice during cooking. Garnish with
orange rind, if desired. Yield: 8 (¾-cup) servings.

PER SERVING: 265 CALORIES (11% FROM FAT)
FAT 3.3G (SATURATED FAT 0.6G)
PROTEIN 2.2G   CARBOHYDRATE 58.3G
CHOLESTEROL 0MG   SODIUM 212MG

FRENCH SILK SOUFFLÉS

Vegetable cooking spray
⅔ cup plus 1 tablespoon sugar, divided
¼ cup all-purpose flour
¼ cup unsweetened cocoa
1 teaspoon instant coffee granules
⅛ teaspoon salt
1 (1-ounce) square semisweet chocolate,
    grated
2 cups evaporated skimmed milk
1 teaspoon vanilla extract
6 egg whites
⅛ teaspoon cream of tartar
2 teaspoons powdered sugar

Coat eight 6-ounce soufflé dishes with cooking
spray; sprinkle evenly with 1 tablespoon sugar.

Combine ⅓ cup sugar, flour, and next 4 ingredients in a medium saucepan, and stir well. Gradually
add milk, stirring constantly with a wire whisk. Bring
mixture to a boil over medium heat; cook, stirring
constantly, 1 minute. Remove from heat, and stir
in vanilla. Pour into a large bowl. Press plastic wrap
onto surface of custard, and cool completely.

Beat egg whites and cream of tartar at high speed
of an electric mixer until foamy. Gradually add
remaining ⅓ cup sugar, 1 tablespoon at a time,
beating mixture until stiff peaks form.

Gently fold egg white mixture into milk mixture.
Spoon mixture evenly into prepared soufflé dishes.
Freeze soufflés until firm (about 2 hours), and wrap
with heavy-duty aluminum foil. Freeze soufflés up
to 2 weeks.

Place frozen soufflés in two 9-inch square baking
pans. Add hot water to pans to a depth of 1 inch.
Bake at 350° for 35 to 40 minutes or until puffy and
set. Sprinkle ¼ teaspoon powdered sugar over each
soufflé. Serve immediately. Yield: 8 soufflés.

PER SOUFFLÉ: 181 CALORIES (9% FROM FAT)
FAT 1.8G (SATURATED FAT 1.0G)
PROTEIN 8.8G   CARBOHYDRATE 32.9G
CHOLESTEROL 3MG   SODIUM 151MG

French Silk Soufflés

Grandma's Simple Roast Chicken and Sweet Potato Cakes

CELEBRATION OF LIGHTS

On this evening of gifts and ritual, you can serve traditional Hanukkah dishes without excess fat and calories. Begin preparation up to three weeks early by baking and freezing the Mandelbrot cookies. Prepare Homemade Applesauce two or three days ahead, chill, and then reheat just before dinner.

Grandma's Simple Roast Chicken

Sweet Potato Cakes

Homemade Applesauce

Mandelbrot

Serves 6

TOTAL CALORIES PER SERVING: 529
(CALORIES FROM FAT: 21%)

GRANDMA'S SIMPLE ROAST CHICKEN

1 (4- to 5-pound) roasting chicken
½ teaspoon salt
½ teaspoon pepper
½ teaspoon paprika
1 medium onion, trimmed and quartered
1 stalk celery, cut into 3-inch pieces
1 medium carrot, cut into 3-inch pieces
1 clove garlic
1 bay leaf
Vegetable cooking spray
Carrot curls (optional)
Celery leaves (optional)

Remove and discard giblets and neck from chicken. Rinse chicken under cold water; pat dry. Trim fat from chicken.

Combine salt, pepper, and paprika; sprinkle over breast, drumsticks, and into body cavity. Place onion and next 4 ingredients in body cavity. Tie ends of legs together with cord. Lift wing tips up and over back; tuck under chicken.

Place chicken, breast side up, on rack of a broiler pan coated with cooking spray. Insert meat thermometer into meaty part of thigh, making sure it does not touch bone. Bake at 400° for 1 hour or until meat thermometer registers 180°. Cover chicken loosely with aluminum foil; let stand 10 minutes. Before serving, remove and discard skin, vegetables, and bay leaf. If desired, garnish with carrot curls and celery leaves. Yield: 8 servings.

PER SERVING: 163 CALORIES (35% FROM FAT)
FAT 6.4G (SATURATED FAT 1.7G)
PROTEIN 24.6G CARBOHYDRATE 0.2G
CHOLESTEROL 76MG SODIUM 220MG

SWEET POTATO CAKES

4 cups peeled, shredded sweet potato (about 1 pound)
¼ cup all-purpose flour
1 teaspoon instant minced onion
⅛ teaspoon salt
⅛ teaspoon pepper
Dash of ground nutmeg
1 egg, lightly beaten
Vegetable cooking spray

Combine all ingredients except cooking spray; stir well.

Coat a large nonstick griddle or skillet with cooking spray. For each cake, spoon about ¼ cup mixture onto hot griddle or skillet; flatten slightly with a spatula. Cook 4 minutes on each side or until golden. Yield: 6 (2-cake) servings.

PER SERVING: 127 CALORIES (9% FROM FAT)
FAT 1.3G (SATURATED FAT 0.3G)
PROTEIN 3.1G CARBOHYDRATE 25.9G
CHOLESTEROL 37MG SODIUM 72MG

HOMEMADE APPLESAUCE

Serve this applesauce warm with
Sweet Potato Cakes or cold as a side dish.

10 cups coarsely chopped red cooking apple (about 3 pounds)
1 cup apple cider
½ cup firmly packed brown sugar

Combine all ingredients in a large saucepan. Bring to a boil. Reduce heat; simmer 1 hour or until apple is tender, stirring occasionally. Yield: 10 (½-cup) servings.

PER SERVING: 118 CALORIES (3% FROM FAT)
FAT 0.4G (SATURATED FAT 0.1G)
PROTEIN 0.2G CARBOHYDRATE 30.4G
CHOLESTEROL 0MG SODIUM 5MG

MANDELBROT

1 cup sugar
⅔ cup vegetable oil
1 (8-ounce) carton fat-free egg substitute
1 tablespoon grated orange rind
1 teaspoon vanilla extract
4½ cups all-purpose flour
1½ tablespoons baking powder
½ teaspoon salt
½ cup finely ground toasted almonds (about 3 ounces)
1 teaspoon ground cinnamon
¼ teaspoon ground cloves
¼ teaspoon ground coriander
¼ teaspoon ground nutmeg
Vegetable cooking spray
Orange Marmalade Frosting (optional)

Combine first 5 ingredients in a large bowl; beat at medium speed of an electric mixer until well blended. Combine flour and next 7 ingredients; gradually add to sugar mixture, beating until well blended. Turn dough out onto a lightly floured surface; knead. Shape dough into 2 (12-inch-long) rolls. Place rolls on a cookie sheet coated with cooking spray; flatten to 1-inch thickness.

Bake at 350° for 20 minutes. Remove rolls from cookie sheet, and cool 10 minutes on a wire rack.

Cut each roll into 24 (½-inch) slices. Place slices, cut sides down, on cookie sheet. Bake at 350° for 10 minutes. Turn cookies over; bake 10 minutes. (Cookies will be slightly soft in center but will harden as they cool.) Remove cookies from cookie sheet, and cool completely on wire rack. Drizzle with Orange Marmalade Frosting, if desired. Yield: 4 dozen.

Note: If desired, make biscotti up to three weeks ahead, and freeze.

ORANGE MARMALADE FROSTING
2 cups sifted powdered sugar
2 tablespoons orange marmalade
1 teaspoon unsweetened orange juice

Position knife blade in food processor bowl; add all ingredients, and process until smooth. Place frosting in a zip-top plastic bag. Snip a tiny hole in one corner of bag; drizzle frosting over biscotti. Yield: 1 cup.

PER COOKIE: 121 CALORIES (30% FROM FAT)
FAT 4.1G (SATURATED FAT 0.7G)
PROTEIN 2.1G   CARBOHYDRATE 19.2G
CHOLESTEROL 0MG   SODIUM 70MG

STAR OF DAVID MANDELBROT

To construct star, divide dough into 3 equal portions; shape each into a quadrilateral that is 9 inches at bottom, 4 inches at top, and 12 inches on each side. Bake at 350° for 20 minutes. Remove from cookie sheet; cool 10 minutes on a wire rack. Beginning at 9-inch bottom, cut each portion into ½-inch-thick slices. Place slices, cut sides down, on cookie sheet; bake at 350° for 10 minutes. Turn cookies over; bake 10 minutes. Drizzle with frosting, if desired; let stand 10 minutes. (Cookies will be slightly soft in center but will harden as they cool.) To assemble star, begin with 3 longest pieces of biscotti, and form a triangle, which is the base of star. Continue to stack biscotti, using longest pieces first. You will have enough biscotti to make 1 large star with 6 layers. Serve remaining biscotti on a tray.

Star of David Mandelbrot

Ragoût of Veal and Mixed Greens with Balsamic Vinaigrette

FESTIVE DINNER PARTY

Take a break from typical holiday fare with this hearty menu featuring a wine-laced ragoût atop fettuccine noodles. It pairs deliciously with the sweet yet tangy salad of greens and a balsamic vinaigrette dressing. After dinner, savor dessert beside the fire with a dressed-up cup of Irish Coffee.

Ragoût of Veal

Mixed Greens with Balsamic Vinaigrette

Cinnamon-Pear Tart

Irish Coffee

Serves 8
TOTAL CALORIES PER SERVING: 779
(CALORIES FROM FAT: 18%)

RAGOÛT OF VEAL

2½ pounds lean boneless veal sirloin tip
    roast
1½ teaspoons paprika
½ teaspoon freshly ground pepper
Vegetable cooking spray
1 tablespoon olive oil, divided
2½ cups sliced leeks
3 cloves garlic, minced
⅓ cup all-purpose flour
1½ cups dry vermouth
2 (14¼-ounce) cans no-salt-added chicken
    broth
2 teaspoons dried thyme
2 bay leaves
1 pound carrots, scraped and cut into
    2-inch-long strips
½ teaspoon salt
8 cups hot cooked fettuccine (cooked without
    salt or fat)
2 tablespoons chopped fresh thyme
Fresh thyme sprigs (optional)

Trim fat from veal; cut veal into 1-inch cubes. Sprinkle paprika and pepper over veal. Coat an ovenproof Dutch oven with cooking spray, and add 1 teaspoon olive oil. Place Dutch oven over medium-high heat until hot. Add half of veal mixture to Dutch oven, and cook until browned on all sides, stirring often. Transfer to a bowl, and set aside. Repeat procedure with 1 teaspoon oil and remaining veal mixture. Wipe drippings from Dutch oven with a paper towel.

Add remaining 1 teaspoon oil to Dutch oven. Place over medium-high heat until hot. Add leeks and garlic; sauté 3 to 4 minutes. Return veal to Dutch oven; sprinkle with flour. Cook, stirring constantly, 1 minute. Stir in vermouth and next 3 ingredients. Bring to a boil; cover and bake at 350° for 30 minutes.

Add carrot and salt to veal mixture, stirring well; bake, uncovered, 35 to 45 minutes or until veal and carrot are tender. Remove and discard bay leaves. Serve over pasta; sprinkle with chopped thyme. Garnish with fresh thyme sprigs, if desired. Yield: 8 servings.

PER SERVING: 439 CALORIES (15% FROM FAT)
FAT 7.2G (SATURATED FAT 1.8G)
PROTEIN 36.1G   CARBOHYDRATE 54.3G
CHOLESTEROL 120MG   SODIUM 325MG

MIXED GREENS WITH BALSAMIC VINAIGRETTE

½ cup canned no-salt-added chicken
    broth
¼ cup balsamic vinegar
1½ tablespoons olive oil
1 tablespoon honey
2 teaspoons coarse-grained mustard
¼ teaspoon salt
1 large clove garlic, minced
1 (6-ounce) package mixed salad greens
7 cups torn Bibb lettuce (2 large heads)
½ teaspoon freshly ground pepper

Combine first 7 ingredients in a bowl. Cover and chill. Combine mixed greens and Bibb lettuce in a large bowl. Add chilled dressing; toss. Arrange evenly on individual salad plates, and sprinkle with pepper. Yield: 8 (1½-cup) servings.

PER SERVING: 43 CALORIES (57% FROM FAT)
FAT 2.7G (SATURATED FAT 0.4G)
PROTEIN 0.9G CARBOHYDRATE 4.0G
CHOLESTEROL 0MG SODIUM 95MG

CINNAMON-PEAR TART

1 cup sifted cake flour
½ cup plus 1 tablespoon sugar, divided
1½ teaspoons ground cinnamon, divided
½ teaspoon baking powder
3 tablespoons chilled stick margarine, cut into
    small pieces
2 to 3 tablespoons ice water
¼ cup all-purpose flour
5 medium pears (about 2 pounds), peeled,
    cored, and thinly sliced
2 cups vanilla nonfat frozen yogurt
Ground cinnamon (optional)

Combine cake flour, 1 tablespoon sugar, ½ teaspoon cinnamon, and baking powder in a bowl; cut in margarine with a pastry blender until mixture resembles coarse meal and is pale yellow (about 3½ minutes). Sprinkle ice water, 1 tablespoon at a time, over surface; toss with a fork until dry ingredients are moistened and mixture is crumbly. (Do not form a ball.)

Gently press mixture into a 4-inch circle on heavy-duty plastic wrap. Cover with additional plastic wrap, and chill at least 15 minutes. Roll dough, still covered, into an 11-inch circle; place in freezer 5 minutes or until plastic wrap can be removed easily.

Remove top sheet of plastic wrap. Invert and fit dough into an ungreased 9-inch tart pan; remove remaining sheet of plastic wrap. Prick bottom of pastry with a fork. Chill 15 minutes. Bake at 400° for 10 minutes or until lightly browned; cool completely on a wire rack.

Combine remaining ½ cup sugar, remaining 1 teaspoon cinnamon, and ¼ cup all-purpose flour in a large bowl. Add pear; toss gently to coat. Let stand at room temperature 15 minutes. Arrange pear in prepared crust. Pour any remaining juices over pear. Bake at 350° for 30 minutes or until pear is tender. Cool completely on a wire rack. Serve with frozen yogurt. Sprinkle with ground cinnamon, if desired. Yield: 8 servings.

PER SERVING: 232 CALORIES (18% FROM FAT)
FAT 4.7G (SATURATED FAT 0.9G)
PROTEIN 3.5G CARBOHYDRATE 45.8G
CHOLESTEROL 0MG SODIUM 91MG

IRISH COFFEE

6 cups strongly brewed coffee
½ cup Irish whiskey
2 tablespoons plus 2 teaspoons sugar
1 cup frozen reduced-calorie whipped topping,
    thawed

Pour ¾ cup brewed coffee into each mug. Add 1 tablespoon Irish whiskey and 1 teaspoon sugar to each mug, stirring until sugar dissolves. Top each serving with 2 tablespoons whipped topping. Serve immediately. Yield: 8 (¾-cup) servings.

PER SERVING: 65 CALORIES (15% FROM FAT)
FAT 1.1G (SATURATED FAT 0.7G)
PROTEIN 0.5G CARBOHYDRATE 8.3G
CHOLESTEROL 0MG SODIUM 10MG

WELCOME CHRISTMAS MORNING

Whatever your Christmas morning tradition, this menu lets you and your family enjoy it to the fullest. The Easy Fruit Compote and the dough for the Cranberry Scones will keep in the refrigerator up to three days. (Menu calories reflect one scone per person.) Chop the vegetables and combine the egg substitute mixture for the frittata the day before. With this advance work, your Christmas morning preparations will be a breeze.

Christmas Frittata

Easy Fruit Compote

Cranberry Scones

Amaretto Cocoa

Serves 4
TOTAL CALORIES PER SERVING: 607
(CALORIES FROM FAT: 12%)

CHRISTMAS FRITTATA

Olive oil-flavored vegetable cooking
   spray
1 tablespoon sliced green onions
2 cloves garlic, minced
1 cup sliced fresh mushrooms
½ cup diced sweet red pepper
¼ cup chopped fresh broccoli
   flowerets
1½ cups fat-free egg substitute
2 tablespoons grated Parmesan
   cheese
½ teaspoon dried basil
¼ teaspoon dried oregano
¼ teaspoon pepper
¼ teaspoon salt
⅛ teaspoon dried crushed red pepper
3 tablespoons crumbled feta cheese

Coat a medium nonstick skillet with cooking spray; place over medium-high heat until hot. Add green onions and garlic; sauté 2 minutes. Add mushrooms, sweet red pepper, and broccoli; sauté 3 minutes.

Combine egg substitute and next 6 ingredients in a bowl, stirring well; pour over vegetable mixture in skillet.

Cover and cook over medium heat 10 minutes or until egg substitute mixture is set. Sprinkle frittata with feta cheese, and serve immediately. Yield: 4 servings.

PER SERVING: 89 CALORIES (24% FROM FAT)
FAT 2.4G (SATURATED FAT 1.4G)
PROTEIN 11.9G CARBOHYDRATE 4.9G
CHOLESTEROL 7MG SODIUM 401MG

Cranberry Scones, Amaretto Cocoa, and Easy Fruit Compote

EASY FRUIT COMPOTE

1 (16-ounce) can pear halves in extra light
  syrup, undrained
1 (20-ounce) can pineapple tidbits in juice,
  undrained
1 (16-ounce) can apricot halves in juice,
  undrained
1 (16-ounce) can sliced peaches in water,
  undrained
¼ cup firmly packed brown sugar
¼ cup unsweetened orange juice
1 tablespoon cornstarch
1 tablespoon fresh lemon juice
4 whole cloves
⅛ teaspoon ground mace
1 (3-inch) stick cinnamon
Additional cinnamon sticks (optional)

Drain canned fruit, reserving ¼ cup liquid from
each can. Discard remaining liquid. Cut pear halves
in half lengthwise. Combine pears, pineapple tidbits, apricot halves, and peaches in a 13- x 9- x 2-
inch baking dish.

Combine reserved liquid, brown sugar, and next
6 ingredients in a saucepan, stirring well. Bring to a
boil over medium heat; reduce heat, and simmer,
uncovered, 2 minutes. Pour over fruit.

Cover and chill at least 8 hours. Bake at 350° for
40 minutes or until thoroughly heated. Remove
and discard cloves and cinnamon stick.

Spoon fruit mixture into a serving bowl. Garnish
with additional cinnamon sticks, if desired. Serve
warm. Yield: 5 (1-cup) servings.

PER SERVING: 190 CALORIES (2% FROM FAT)
FAT 0.5G (SATURATED FAT 0.0G)
PROTEIN 1.7G   CARBOHYDRATE 48.4G
CHOLESTEROL 0MG   SODIUM 21MG

CRANBERRY SCONES

2 cups all-purpose flour
1 tablespoon baking powder
¼ teaspoon baking soda
⅓ cup sugar
2 tablespoons chilled stick margarine, cut into
    small pieces
⅓ cup dried cranberries
1 cup nonfat buttermilk
1 tablespoon vanilla extract
Vegetable cooking spray
3 tablespoons chopped walnuts
1½ teaspoons sugar

Combine first 4 ingredients in a large bowl; cut
in margarine with a pastry blender until mixture
resembles coarse meal. Stir in cranberries. Add
buttermilk and vanilla, stirring just until moistened.

Drop dough by 2 heaping tablespoonfuls, 2
inches apart, onto cookie sheets coated with cooking spray. Sprinkle evenly with walnuts and 1½
teaspoons sugar. Bake at 400° for 15 to 17 minutes
or until golden. Yield: 1 dozen.

PER SCONE: 153 CALORIES (21% FROM FAT)
FAT 3.6G (SATURATED FAT 0.6G)
PROTEIN 3.5G   CARBOHYDRATE 26.3G
CHOLESTEROL 1MG   SODIUM 171MG

AMARETTO COCOA

¼ cup plus 2 tablespoons sugar
3 tablespoons unsweetened cocoa
⅛ teaspoon salt
1⅔ cups water
1 cup evaporated skimmed milk
1 cup low-fat milk
1 tablespoon amaretto

Combine first 3 ingredients in a saucepan. Stir in
water. Bring to a boil; add milks and amaretto.
Cook until heated. Yield: 4 (1-cup) servings.

PER SERVING: 175 CALORIES (10% FROM FAT)
FAT 1.9G (SATURATED FAT 1.2G)
PROTEIN 8.1G   CARBOHYDRATE 31.7G
CHOLESTEROL 5MG   SODIUM 183MG

Crab Quiche Florentine, Spiced Winter Fruit, and Cinnamon-Streusel Coffee Cake

EASY HOLIDAY BRUNCH

Make the brunch morning easier by baking and freezing the coffee cake two weeks ahead. Thaw the cake and prepare and chill the fruit and the spinach mixture for the quiche a day ahead. On brunch morning, assemble and bake the quiche, and prepare the easy spritzer.

Crab Quiche Florentine

Spiced Winter Fruit

Cinnamon-Streusel Coffee Cake

Cranberry-Raspberry Spritzers

Serves 6
TOTAL CALORIES PER SERVING: 676
(CALORIES FROM FAT: 20%)

CRAB QUICHE FLORENTINE

*Place the pieplate on a baking sheet in
case the filling bubbles over.*

1 (7-ounce) can refrigerated breadstick dough
Vegetable cooking spray
¾ cup (3 ounces) shredded Gruyère cheese
8 ounces lump crabmeat, shell pieces removed
   and drained
½ cup chopped onion
4 cups coarsely chopped spinach
⅛ teaspoon dried tarragon
⅛ teaspoon Old Bay seasoning
⅛ teaspoon ground nutmeg
⅛ teaspoon pepper
1 cup evaporated skimmed milk
½ cup fat-free egg substitute
Cherry tomatoes, quartered (optional)

Unroll dough, separating into strips. Working on a flat surface, coil 1 strip of dough around itself in a spiral pattern. Add second strip of dough to end of first strip, pinching ends together to seal; continue coiling dough. Repeat procedure with remaining dough strips. Cover dough with a towel; let rest 20 minutes. Roll dough into a 13-inch circle; fit into a 9-inch pieplate coated with cooking spray. Fold edges under; flute. Sprinkle cheese over bottom of crust. Top with crabmeat; set aside.

Coat a large nonstick skillet with cooking spray; place over medium-high heat. Add onion; sauté 4 minutes. Add spinach and next 4 ingredients; cook 2 minutes or until spinach wilts. Arrange spinach mixture over crabmeat.

Combine milk and egg substitute; stir well with a wire whisk. Pour over spinach mixture. Bake at 375° for 45 minutes or until a knife inserted in center comes out clean; let stand 10 minutes. Garnish with cherry tomatoes, if desired. Yield: 6 servings.

Note: Cook spinach mixture, and then chill overnight, if desired.

PER SERVING: 248 CALORIES (29% FROM FAT)
FAT 7.7G (SATURATED FAT 3.7G)
PROTEIN 20.8G   CARBOHYDRATE 23.2G
CHOLESTEROL 55MG   SODIUM 556MG

HAM AND CHEESE QUICHE

Substitute Swiss cheese for Gruyère cheese, and ¾ cup chopped reduced-fat, low-salt ham (about ¼ pound) for crabmeat. Omit spinach, tarragon, Old Bay seasoning, and nutmeg; add ⅛ teaspoon salt. Cook ham, onion, salt, and pepper 4 minutes in a skillet coated with cooking spray. Proceed as directed. Yield: 6 servings.

PER SERVING: 220 CALORIES (30% FROM FAT)
FAT 7.2G (SATURATED FAT 3.4G)
PROTEIN 15.3G   CARBOHYDRATE 22.6G
CHOLESTEROL 24MG   SODIUM 557MG

SPICED WINTER FRUIT

*Turn to page 88 for directions
on sectioning grapefruit.*

2 large pink grapefruit
⅓ cup small pitted prunes
⅓ cup dried figs, cut into quarters
3 tablespoons light brown sugar
7 whole cloves
1 (3-inch) stick cinnamon
1 cup seedless red grapes, halved

Peel and section grapefruit over a bowl; squeeze membranes to extract juice. Set sections aside; reserve juice, and add water to measure 1¼ cups.

Combine juice mixture, prunes, and next 4 ingredients in a saucepan; bring to a boil. Reduce heat; simmer 15 minutes, stirring occasionally. Remove from heat; cool. Remove and discard cloves and cinnamon stick. Stir in grapefruit sections and grapes. Yield: 8 (½-cup) servings.

PER SERVING: 97 CALORIES (3% FROM FAT)
FAT 0.3G (SATURATED FAT 0.0G)
PROTEIN 1.1G   CARBOHYDRATE 25.0G
CHOLESTEROL 0MG   SODIUM 3MG

CINNAMON-STREUSEL COFFEE CAKE

Soften brown sugar that's hard and dry by microwaving it for a few seconds.

⅓ cup chopped walnuts
⅓ cup firmly packed brown sugar
3 tablespoons all-purpose flour
1 tablespoon ground cinnamon
Vegetable cooking spray
1¼ cups sugar
⅓ cup vegetable oil
2 eggs
3 cups all-purpose flour
1 teaspoon baking powder
1 teaspoon baking soda
½ teaspoon salt
1½ cups low-fat buttermilk
1 tablespoon vanilla extract

Combine first 4 ingredients; stir well. Coat a 12-cup Bundt pan with cooking spray; sprinkle ⅓ cup walnut mixture into pan. Set remaining walnut mixture aside.

Combine 1¼ cups sugar and oil in a large bowl; beat at medium speed of an electric mixer until well blended. Add eggs, one at a time, beating well after each addition. Combine flour and next 3 ingredients, stirring well. Add flour mixture to creamed mixture alternately with buttermilk, beginning and ending with flour mixture; mix after each addition. Stir in vanilla.

Set aside 2 cups batter. Pour remaining batter into prepared pan; sprinkle reserved walnut mixture over batter in pan. Pour reserved 2 cups batter over walnut mixture. Bake at 350° for 45 minutes or until a wooden pick inserted in center comes out clean. Cool in pan on a wire rack 10 minutes; remove from pan. Cool completely on wire rack. Yield: 16 servings.

PER SERVING: 249 CALORIES (26% FROM FAT)
FAT 7.3G (SATURATED FAT 1.4G)
PROTEIN 4.9G CARBOHYDRATE 41.1G
CHOLESTEROL 28MG SODIUM 200MG

CRANBERRY-RASPBERRY SPRITZERS

To garnish, thread fresh cranberries and fresh lemon slices onto wooden skewers.

3 cups unsweetened raspberry-flavored sparkling water, chilled
3 cups cranberry-raspberry juice drink, chilled
¼ plus 2 tablespoons crème de cassis or other black currant-flavored liqueur, divided

Combine sparkling water and cranberry-raspberry juice drink in a pitcher; stir well. Spoon 1 tablespoon crème de cassis into each of six glasses; add 1 cup juice mixture to each glass. Yield: 6 (1-cup) servings.

PER SERVING: 82 CALORIES (0% FROM FAT)
FAT 0.0G (SATURATED FAT 0.0G)
PROTEIN 0.4G CARBOHYDRATE 16.5G
CHOLESTEROL 0MG SODIUM 3MG

Cranberry-Raspberry Spritzer

NEW YEAR'S EVE GALA

For your New Year's Eve get-together, try this cocktail buffet. These big-flavored recipes include dips, biscuit sandwiches, turnovers, tartlets, and even a red wine glögg. And you can make most of them in advance. (Analysis per serving includes one serving each of the glögg and shrimp, one of each appetizer, three baby carrots, three strawberries, and one tablespoon of each dip.)

Holiday Glögg

Deviled Dip

Buffalo Shrimp with Blue Cheese Dip

Cranberry Biscuits with Smoked Turkey

Curried Mushroom Turnovers

Fluffy Fruit Dip with Almond Chips and fresh fruit

Lemon-Macaroon Tartlets

Serves 12
TOTAL CALORIES PER SERVING: 614
(CALORIES FROM FAT: 19%)

HOLIDAY GLÖGG

*This lightened version of a traditional Swedish
holiday punch will take the chill off winter nights.*

3½ cups water
1 tablespoon whole cloves
¼ teaspoon ground cardamom
2 (3-inch) sticks cinnamon
2 (750-milliliter) bottles dry red
    wine
1 cup raisins
1 cup sugar

Combine first 4 ingredients in a large saucepan; bring mixture to a boil. Reduce heat, and simmer 20 minutes.

Strain liquid through a sieve into a bowl; remove and discard cloves and cinnamon sticks. Return liquid to saucepan. Stir in wine, raisins, and sugar; cook over medium heat just until sugar is dissolved and mixture is thoroughly heated, stirring occasionally. Serve warm. Yield: 18 (½-cup) servings.

Note: Substitute nonalcoholic dry red wine for regular wine, if desired.

PER SERVING: 72 CALORIES (0% FROM FAT)
FAT 0.0G (SATURATED FAT 0.0G)
PROTEIN 0.4G CARBOHYDRATE 18.6G
CHOLESTEROL 0MG   SODIUM 7MG

Buffalo Shrimp with Blue Cheese Dip, Cranberry Biscuits with Smoked Turkey, and Curried Mushroom Turnovers

DEVILED DIP

1 cup minced red onion
Vegetable cooking spray
1 tablespoon sugar
2 tablespoons water
1 tablespoon white wine vinegar
1½ cups 1% low-fat cottage cheese
¼ cup nonfat mayonnaise
1 teaspoon hot sauce
¼ teaspoon salt
¼ teaspoon chili powder
⅛ teaspoon garlic powder

Sauté onion in a skillet coated with cooking spray over medium-high heat until tender. Stir in sugar, water, and vinegar. Cover; cook 1 minute. Remove from heat; cool. Process cheese in food processor until smooth. Combine cheese, onion mixture, mayonnaise, and remaining ingredients. Cover; chill. Serve with raw vegetables. Yield: 2 cups.

PER TABLESPOON: 13 CALORIES (7% FROM FAT)
FAT 0.1G (SATURATED FAT 0.1G)
PROTEIN 1.4G CARBOHYDRATE 1.5G
CHOLESTEROL 0MG SODIUM 87MG

Party Timetable

- **Two weeks ahead:** Write out grocery lists—one for items to purchase then and one for perishables to purchase three days ahead.
- **Two to three days ahead:** Make dips and bake tart shells. Cover and chill all.
- **One day ahead:** Prepare filling for tartlets, vegetables for dip, and beverage; cover and chill all. Buy shrimp.
- **Early on New Year's Eve:** Prepare fruit (use citric acid solution to prevent browning). Peel and devein shrimp; prepare marinade. Assemble tartlets. Cover and chill all. Make biscuits and turnovers.
- **One hour ahead:** Marinate shrimp 30 minutes. Reheat turnovers and biscuits. Broil shrimp. Fill biscuits with turkey.

BUFFALO SHRIMP WITH BLUE CHEESE DIP

48 unpeeled large fresh shrimp (about 2 pounds)
2 tablespoons dark brown sugar
2 tablespoons chopped onion
3 tablespoons cider vinegar
2 tablespoons water
2 tablespoons ketchup
1 tablespoon Worcestershire sauce
2 to 4 teaspoons hot sauce
¼ teaspoon pepper
1 clove garlic, chopped
¾ cup fat-free cottage cheese
3 tablespoons fat-free milk
2 tablespoons (½ ounce) crumbled blue cheese
⅛ teaspoon pepper
Vegetable cooking spray
Celery sticks and leaves (optional)

Peel and devein shrimp, leaving tails intact. Place shrimp in a shallow dish; cover and chill.

Combine sugar and next 8 ingredients in container of an electric blender; cover and process until smooth. Pour sugar mixture into a saucepan. Cook over medium-low heat 10 minutes, stirring occasionally. Cool; pour over shrimp. Cover and marinate in refrigerator 30 minutes, turning occasionally.

Combine cottage cheese and next 3 ingredients in blender; cover and process until smooth. Spoon into a bowl; cover and chill.

Remove shrimp from marinade, reserving marinade. Arrange shrimp in a single layer on rack of a broiler pan coated with cooking spray; broil 5½ inches from heat (with electric oven door partially opened) 3 minutes. Turn shrimp over; baste with reserved marinade. Broil 3 additional minutes or until shrimp turn pink. Serve with cheese dip; garnish with celery sticks and leaves, if desired. Yield: 16 appetizer servings.

Note: Each appetizer serving includes 3 shrimp and 1 tablespoon dip.

PER SERVING: 78 CALORIES (14% FROM FAT)
FAT 1.2G (SATURATED FAT 0.4G)
PROTEIN 13.0G CARBOHYDRATE 3.2G
CHOLESTEROL 84MG SODIUM 173MG

CRANBERRY BISCUITS WITH SMOKED TURKEY

These biscuits are a breeze to make in a food processor; you can also make them by hand.

2 cups bread flour
1 teaspoon baking powder
¼ teaspoon salt
2 tablespoons shortening
3 tablespoons sugar
1 package active dry yeast
⅔ cup warm low-fat buttermilk (105° to 115°)
2 tablespoons warm water (105° to 115°)
½ cup dried cranberries
Vegetable cooking spray
1 pound thinly sliced smoked turkey breast
Spicy mustard (optional)

Position knife blade in food processor bowl; add first 3 ingredients, and pulse 2 times or until blended. Add shortening; process 10 seconds or until blended. Combine sugar and next 3 ingredients in a small bowl, stirring to dissolve yeast; let stand 5 minutes. With processor running, slowly pour yeast mixture through food chute; process until dough forms a ball.

Turn dough out onto a lightly floured surface; knead in cranberries. Roll dough to ½-inch thickness; cut into 20 rounds with a 2-inch biscuit cutter. Place rounds on a baking sheet coated with cooking spray. Let rise, uncovered, in a warm place (85°), free from drafts, 20 minutes or until puffy.

Bake at 425° for 8 minutes or until golden. Split biscuits; fill each with ¾ ounce turkey. Serve with mustard, if desired. Yield: 20 appetizers.

PER APPETIZER: 108 CALORIES (17% FROM FAT)
FAT 2.0G (SATURATED FAT 0.0G)
PROTEIN 7.4G CARBOHYDRATE 15.3G
CHOLESTEROL 13MG SODIUM 209MG

CURRIED MUSHROOM TURNOVERS

1 cup mango chutney
½ cup plain low-fat yogurt
Butter-flavored vegetable cooking spray
5¼ cups minced fresh mushrooms
1¼ cups minced shallot
3 tablespoons all-purpose flour
1½ teaspoons curry powder
¾ teaspoon salt
¾ teaspoon ground cumin
¾ teaspoon pepper
½ cup plain low-fat yogurt
2 tablespoons chopped fresh cilantro
12 sheets frozen phyllo pastry, thawed

Combine chutney and ½ cup yogurt. Cover and chill.

Place a large nonstick skillet coated with cooking spray over medium-high heat until hot. Add mushrooms and shallot to skillet; sauté 10 minutes or until mixture appears dry. Combine flour and next 4 ingredients; add to skillet. Cook, stirring constantly, 3 minutes. Remove from heat; add ½ cup yogurt and cilantro, stirring well.

Working with 1 phyllo sheet at a time (cover remaining dough to keep from drying), cut sheet in half lengthwise, and lightly coat with cooking spray. Fold phyllo piece in half lengthwise to form a strip. Spoon 1 tablespoon mushroom mixture onto 1 end of phyllo strip, and fold left bottom corner over mushroom mixture, forming a triangle. Keep folding back and forth into a triangle to end of strip. Repeat procedure with remaining phyllo sheets and mushroom mixture.

Place triangles, seam sides down, on baking sheets. Lightly coat triangles with cooking spray; bake at 400° for 10 minutes or until turnovers are golden. Serve each turnover warm with 1 tablespoon chutney sauce. Yield: 24 appetizer servings.

PER SERVING: 80 CALORIES (15% FROM FAT)
FAT 1.3G (SATURATED FAT 0.2G)
PROTEIN 2.0G CARBOHYDRATE 15.7G
CHOLESTEROL 1MG SODIUM 151MG

FLUFFY FRUIT DIP WITH ALMOND CHIPS

¼ cup low-fat sour cream
¼ cup peach preserves
1 (7-ounce) jar marshmallow creme
¼ cup almond brickle chips

Combine first 3 ingredients in a bowl, stirring with a wire whisk until blended. Cover and chill at least 2 hours or up to 2 days. Stir in brickle chips just before serving. Serve with assorted fruit. Yield: 1½ cups.

PER TABLESPOON: 51 CALORIES (21% FROM FAT)
FAT 1.2G (SATURATED FAT 0.5G)
PROTEIN 0.2G   CARBOHYDRATE 10.5G
CHOLESTEROL 2MG   SODIUM 21MG

LEMON-MACAROON TARTLETS

¾ cup sugar
1 tablespoon plus 2 teaspoons cornstarch
½ teaspoon grated lemon rind
⅓ cup water
⅓ cup fresh lemon juice
1 egg, lightly beaten
2 drops yellow food coloring (optional)
Macaroon Tart Shells
½ cup frozen reduced-calorie whipped topping, thawed
2 tablespoons flaked sweetened coconut, toasted

Combine first 3 ingredients in a saucepan. Gradually add water and lemon juice, stirring with a wire whisk until blended. Bring to a boil over medium heat; cook, stirring constantly, 1 minute. Gradually stir one-fourth of hot lemon mixture into egg; add to remaining lemon mixture, stirring constantly. Cook over medium heat, stirring constantly, 1 minute or until thickened. Pour into a bowl; stir in food coloring, if desired. Place plastic wrap on surface, and chill.

Spoon 1 heaping tablespoon lemon mixture into each Macaroon Tart Shell. Top each with 2 teaspoons whipped topping, and sprinkle with ½ teaspoon toasted coconut. Yield: 12 servings.
Note: If lemon mixture is stored overnight before being placed in tart shells, increase cornstarch to 2 tablespoons.

MACAROON TART SHELLS
2 cups flaked sweetened coconut
½ cup sugar
¼ cup plus 2 tablespoons all-purpose flour
1 teaspoon vanilla extract
2 egg whites, lightly beaten
Vegetable cooking spray

Combine all ingredients except cooking spray in a bowl; spoon mixture evenly into muffin pans coated with cooking spray, pressing mixture into bottom and up sides of muffin cups. Bake at 400° for 15 minutes or until edges are browned. Cool in pans on wire racks 2 minutes. Remove from pans; cool completely on wire racks. Yield: 1 dozen.

PER TARTLET: 198 CALORIES (31% FROM FAT)
FAT 6.8G (SATURATED FAT 5.6G)
PROTEIN 2.1G   CARBOHYDRATE 33.5G
CHOLESTEROL 18MG   SODIUM 62MG

Lemon-Macaroon Tartlet

Honey-Dijon Pork Tenderloin

HAPPY NEW YEAR BUFFET

Invite friends to a buffet featuring "good luck" foods with a twist. Make it easier by preparing the beverage, salad dressing, and roll dough ahead. (Analysis reflects one roll per serving.)

Scarlet Sipper

Honey-Dijon Pork Tenderloin

Spicy Black-Eyed Peas

Spinach-Orange Salad

Cornmeal Crescent Rolls

Maple-Pecan Cheesecake

Serves 12
TOTAL CALORIES PER SERVING: 805
(CALORIES FROM FAT: 23%)

SCARLET SIPPER

1 (48-ounce) bottle cranberry-apple juice
    cocktail
1⅔ cups unsweetened orange juice
¼ cup lemon juice
3 (11-ounce) bottles sparkling mineral water,
    chilled

Combine first 3 ingredients in a large pitcher; stir well. Chill thoroughly. Stir in mineral water just before serving. Yield: 12 (1-cup) servings.

PER SERVING: 93 CALORIES (0% FROM FAT)
FAT 0.0G (SATURATED FAT 0.0G)
PROTEIN 0.4G   CARBOHYDRATE 23.5G
CHOLESTEROL 0MG   SODIUM 19MG

HONEY-DIJON PORK TENDERLOIN

4 (¾-pound) pork tenderloins
½ teaspoon salt
¼ teaspoon pepper
Vegetable cooking spray
1 tablespoon olive oil
½ cup balsamic vinegar
1 tablespoon minced fresh rosemary
3 tablespoons honey
1 tablespoon Dijon mustard
Fresh rosemary sprigs (optional)

Trim fat from pork; sprinkle pork with salt and pepper. Coat a large nonstick skillet with cooking spray; add oil. Place over medium-high heat until hot. Add 2 tenderloins; cook 10 minutes or until browned, turning occasionally. Remove from skillet, and keep warm. Repeat procedure with remaining pork.

Place pork on a rack in a roasting pan coated with cooking spray. Combine vinegar and next 3 ingredients, stirring well; brush over pork. Insert a meat thermometer into thickest part of pork, if desired.

Bake at 400° for 25 to 30 minutes or until meat thermometer registers 160°, basting often with vinegar mixture. Let stand 10 minutes; cut into thin slices. Transfer to a serving platter; garnish with fresh rosemary sprigs, if desired. Yield: 12 servings.

PER SERVING: 160 CALORIES (28% FROM FAT)
FAT 5.0G (SATURATED FAT 1.5G)
PROTEIN 22.6G   CARBOHYDRATE 5.1G
CHOLESTEROL 73MG   SODIUM 188MG

SPICY BLACK-EYED PEAS

3¾ cups frozen black-eyed peas
2½ cups water
Vegetable cooking spray
1¼ cups chopped onion
1¼ cups chopped green pepper
2 (14½-ounce) cans no-salt-added stewed
    tomatoes, undrained and chopped
2 tablespoons low-sodium soy sauce
2 teaspoons dry mustard
1 teaspoon chili powder
1 teaspoon pepper
2 teaspoons liquid smoke
¼ teaspoon ground red pepper
2 tablespoons minced fresh parsley

Combine black-eyed peas and water in a saucepan. Bring to a boil; cover, reduce heat, and simmer 20 minutes. Drain; set aside.

Coat a nonstick skillet with cooking spray; place over medium heat until hot. Add onion and green pepper; sauté until crisp-tender. Add peas, tomato, and next 6 ingredients. Bring to a boil; reduce heat, and simmer 20 minutes or until peas are tender, stirring occasionally. Transfer to a serving dish; sprinkle with parsley. Serve with a slotted spoon. Yield: 12 (¾-cup) servings.

PER SERVING: 99 CALORIES (5% FROM FAT)
FAT 0.6G (SATURATED FAT 0.1G)
PROTEIN 5.4G   CARBOHYDRATE 18.8G
CHOLESTEROL 0MG   SODIUM 83MG

SPINACH-ORANGE SALAD

1 pound fresh spinach, washed and trimmed
6 medium oranges, peeled and sectioned
2 (6-ounce) cans sliced water chestnuts, drained
2 cups sliced fresh mushrooms
½ cup thinly sliced green onions
Yogurt-Poppy Seed Dressing

Combine first 5 ingredients; toss gently. To serve, arrange spinach mixture evenly on 12 individual salad plates; top each salad with 1½ tablespoons Yogurt-Poppy Seed Dressing. Yield: 12 servings.

YOGURT-POPPY SEED DRESSING

½ cup plain nonfat yogurt
¼ cup plus 2 tablespoons nonfat mayonnaise
2 tablespoons honey
2 tablespoons fat-free milk
2 teaspoons poppy seeds
1 teaspoon grated orange rind

Combine all ingredients in a small bowl; stir well. Cover and chill thoroughly. Yield: 1 cup.

PER SERVING: 86 CALORIES (5% FROM FAT)
FAT 0.5G (SATURATED FAT 0.1G)
PROTEIN 2.7G   CARBOHYDRATE 19.2G
CHOLESTEROL 0MG   SODIUM 129MG

CORNMEAL CRESCENT ROLLS

1 package active dry yeast
⅛ teaspoon sugar
½ cup warm water (105° to 115°)
1 cup whole wheat flour
⅓ cup yellow cornmeal
3 tablespoons instant nonfat dry milk powder
½ cup plain nonfat yogurt
¼ cup vegetable oil
2 tablespoons molasses
½ teaspoon salt
1¼ cups plus 3 tablespoons bread flour, divided
Vegetable cooking spray
1 egg white, lightly beaten
1 teaspoon water

Combine first 3 ingredients in a large bowl; let stand 5 minutes. Add whole wheat flour and next 6 ingredients; beat at medium speed of an electric mixer until well blended. Stir in enough of 1¼ cups bread flour to make a soft dough.

Sprinkle 1 tablespoon bread flour over work surface. Turn dough out onto floured surface; knead until smooth and elastic (8 to 10 minutes). Place dough in a bowl coated with cooking spray; turn to coat top. Cover and let rise in a warm place (85°), free from drafts, 1 hour or until doubled in bulk.

Sprinkle 1 tablespoon bread flour over work surface. Punch dough down; divide in half. Roll 1 portion of dough into a 12-inch circle; coat top of dough with cooking spray. Cut circle into 12 wedges. Roll up wedges, beginning at wide end; seal points. Place rolls, point sides down, 2 inches apart on baking sheets coated with cooking spray. Curve rolls into crescents. Repeat procedure. Cover with plastic wrap, and chill 2 to 24 hours.

Combine egg white and 1 teaspoon water; stir. Uncover dough; brush egg white mixture over rolls. Bake at 375° for 10 to 12 minutes. Yield: 2 dozen.

PER ROLL: 85 CALORIES (28% FROM FAT)
FAT 2.6G (SATURATED FAT 0.5G)
PROTEIN 2.7G   CARBOHYDRATE 13.0G
CHOLESTEROL 0MG   SODIUM 61MG

MAPLE-PECAN CHEESECAKE

⅔ cup graham cracker crumbs
2 tablespoons sugar
1 tablespoon stick margarine, melted
½ teaspoon ground cinnamon
Vegetable cooking spray
2 (8-ounce) blocks ⅓-less-fat cream cheese, softened
2 (8-ounce) blocks nonfat cream cheese, softened
2 tablespoons cornstarch
¼ teaspoon salt
1¼ cups maple syrup
3 egg whites
¼ cup chopped pecans, toasted
1 pecan half (optional)
Flowering mint sprig (optional)

Maple-Pecan Cheesecake

Combine first 4 ingredients; toss with a fork until blended. Press crumb mixture into bottom of an 8-inch springform pan coated with cooking spray. Bake at 400° for 8 minutes. Cool on a wire rack.

Combine cheeses, cornstarch, and salt in a large bowl; beat at high speed of an electric mixer until smooth. Gradually add maple syrup, beating well. Add egg whites; beat just until well blended.

Pour half of cheese mixture into prepared crust, and sprinkle with chopped pecans. Top with remaining cheese mixture. Bake at 525° for 7 minutes. Reduce oven temperature to 200° (do not remove pan from oven); bake 45 minutes or until almost set.

Remove cheesecake from oven; cool to room temperature. Cover and chill at least 8 hours. Garnish with pecan half and mint sprig, if desired. Yield: 12 servings.

PER SERVING: 282 CALORIES (39% FROM FAT)
FAT 12.2G (SATURATED FAT 5.9G)
PROTEIN 10.5G CARBOHYDRATE 32.6G
CHOLESTEROL 35MG SODIUM 489MG

Orange-Lime Margaritas (recipe on page 41) and Roasted Pepper Dip (recipe on page 42)

FESTIVE BEGINNINGS

Parties make the holidays memorable, and tempting hors d'oeuvres make the parties outstanding. This chapter includes an assortment of irresistible appetizers and beverages that are surprisingly low in fat. Choose one or two for an appetizer before dinner, or go with several for an open-house buffet.

To accommodate your holiday schedule, you can prepare many of these recipes ahead. In fact, Shrimp-Chutney Spread (page 44) and Smoked Turkey and Sun-Dried Tomato Pâté (page 45) are best if served very cold. For a hot appetizer, assemble Hot Artichoke Dip (page 42) or Spinach-Ham Dip (page 43) early in the day; then bake just before serving.

You can even make the fruit drinks and punches, such as Sparkling Cranberry Blush (page 41), a day or two before the party. All you have to do at the last minute is stir in the champagne or sparkling water. Just remember to chill these last-minute additions thoroughly when adding them to the previously chilled portion of the recipe.

MULLED FRUIT DRINK

2 cups water
6 whole cloves
3 (3-inch) sticks cinnamon
8 regular-size tea bags
2½ cups unsweetened pineapple juice
2 cups unsweetened apple juice
½ cup lemon juice
½ cup sugar
Lemon wedges (optional)

Combine first 3 ingredients in a 1-quart glass measuring cup. Microwave at HIGH 5 minutes or until boiling. Pour over tea bags in a 2-quart glass measuring cup. Cover and let stand 10 minutes. Remove and discard spices and tea bags. Stir in juices and sugar. Microwave, uncovered, at HIGH 8 minutes or until hot, stirring halfway through cooking time. Pour into mugs, and garnish with lemon wedges, if desired. Yield: 7 (1-cup) servings.

PER SERVING: 144 CALORIES (1% FROM FAT)
FAT 0.1G (SATURATED FAT 0.0G)
PROTEIN 0.4G   CARBOHYDRATE 36.6G
CHOLESTEROL 0MG   SODIUM 5MG

Mulled Fruit Drink

SPICED FRUIT TEA

2 cups unsweetened orange juice
2 cups unsweetened pineapple juice
¼ cup honey
¾ teaspoon whole cloves
¼ teaspoon whole allspice
2 (3-inch) sticks cinnamon, broken in half
2 cups water
3 regular-size tea bags
Orange wedges studded with cloves (optional)

Combine first 3 ingredients in a saucepan, stirring well. Place ¾ teaspoon cloves, allspice, and cinnamon sticks on a 6-inch square of cheesecloth; tie with string. Add spice bag to fruit juice mixture. Bring to a boil; cover, reduce heat, and simmer 30 minutes. Remove and discard spice bag.

Bring 2 cups water to a boil in a saucepan. Add tea bags; remove from heat. Cover and let stand 15 minutes. Remove and discard tea bags. Combine tea and juice mixture, stirring well. Serve warm. Garnish with orange wedges studded with cloves, if desired. Yield: 6 (1-cup) servings.

PER SERVING: 128 CALORIES (1% FROM FAT)
FAT 0.1G (SATURATED FAT 0.0G)
PROTEIN 0.9G   CARBOHYDRATE 32.4G
CHOLESTEROL 0MG   SODIUM 2MG

Remember the Garnish

Make your holiday foods more festive by adding creative garnishes. When garnishing a beverage, select an ingredient already in the drink or one that complements the drink. Long cinnamon sticks are often appropriate for hot, fruit juice-based drinks—the sticks even serve double-duty as stirrers. For cold beverages, skewer fruit onto wooden picks to make colorful, edible stirrers.

Spiked Cranberry-Apple Cider

SPIKED CRANBERRY-APPLE CIDER

4 cups cranberry-apple juice drink
¼ cup frozen lemonade concentrate, thawed
    and undiluted
3 tablespoons sugar
2 (3-inch) sticks cinnamon
½ teaspoon whole cloves
¼ teaspoon whole allspice
¼ cup light rum
Additional cinnamon sticks (optional)
Lemon slices studded with cloves (optional)

Combine first 3 ingredients in a large saucepan. Place 2 cinnamon sticks, ½ teaspoon cloves, and allspice on a small piece of cheesecloth; tie with string. Add to cranberry-apple drink mixture. Bring mixture to a boil; cover, reduce heat, and simmer 10 minutes.

Remove from heat. Remove and discard spice bag. Stir in rum. If desired, garnish with additional cinnamon sticks and lemon slices studded with cloves. Yield: 6 (¾-cup) servings.

PER SERVING: 178 CALORIES (0% FROM FAT)
FAT 0.0G (SATURATED FAT 0.0G)
PROTEIN 0.2G   CARBOHYDRATE 39.9G
CHOLESTEROL 0MG   SODIUM 4MG

ORANGE TWIST

For a nonalcoholic version, omit rum and add 1½ cups orange juice to cranberry-apple drink mixture before bringing to a boil. Yield: 6 (1-cup) servings.

PER SERVING: 184 CALORIES (0% FROM FAT)
FAT 0.1G (SATURATED FAT 0.1G)
PROTEIN 0.6G   CARBOHYDRATE 46.6G
CHOLESTEROL 0MG   SODIUM 4MG

HOT MULLED WINE

1 cup water
1 cup unsweetened apple juice
1 cup unsweetened orange juice
⅓ cup sugar
2 teaspoons whole cloves
4 (3-inch) sticks cinnamon
6 slices lemon
6 slices orange
5 cups dry red wine
Additional cinnamon sticks (optional)

Combine first 4 ingredients in a nonaluminum saucepan; stir well. Place cloves and 4 cinnamon sticks on a piece of cheesecloth; tie with string. Add cheesecloth bag to juice mixture. Bring mixture to a boil; reduce heat, and simmer 10 minutes, stirring occasionally. Remove from heat; add lemon and orange slices. Cover; let stand 15 minutes.

Add wine to juice mixture; stir well. Bring mixture almost to a boil (do not boil). Remove and discard cheesecloth bag and fruit slices. Pour into mugs; garnish with additional cinnamon sticks, if desired. Yield: 10 (¾-cup) servings.

PER SERVING: 55 CALORIES (0% FROM FAT)
FAT 0.0G (SATURATED FAT 0.0G)
PROTEIN 0.4G   CARBOHYDRATE 13.8G
CHOLESTEROL 0MG   SODIUM 10MG

COFFEE ROYALE

1¼ cups low-fat milk
1 tablespoon sugar
¼ teaspoon ground cinnamon
2¾ cups hot strongly brewed coffee
½ cup amaretto or other almond-flavored
    liqueur
Cinnamon sticks (optional)

Combine first 3 ingredients in a saucepan; stir well. Cook, stirring constantly, over medium heat 2 minutes or until sugar dissolves. Remove from heat; stir in coffee and amaretto. Pour into mugs; garnish with cinnamon sticks, if desired. Yield: 6 (¾-cup) servings.
  Nonalcoholic version: Omit amaretto, and increase coffee to 3¼ cups.

PER SERVING: 96 CALORIES (6% FROM FAT)
FAT 0.6G (SATURATED FAT 0.4G)
PROTEIN 1.8G CARBOHYDRATE 10.9G
CHOLESTEROL 2MG SODIUM 28MG

COFFEE-KAHLÚA PUNCH

8¼ cups hot strongly brewed coffee
⅓ cup sugar
4 cups fat-free milk
1 tablespoon vanilla extract
1¼ cups Kahlúa or other coffee-flavored
    liqueur
5 cups vanilla nonfat ice cream, softened
1 (1-ounce) square semisweet chocolate,
    coarsely grated

Combine coffee and sugar, stirring until sugar dissolves. Stir in milk and vanilla; cover and chill. Combine chilled coffee mixture and Kahlúa in a punch bowl; stir well. Spoon tablespoons of ice cream into coffee mixture; stir until ice cream melts. Sprinkle with chocolate. Serve immediately. Yield: 18 (1-cup) servings.

PER SERVING: 150 CALORIES (13% FROM FAT)
FAT 2.2G (SATURATED FAT 1.4G)
PROTEIN 3.4G CARBOHYDRATE 21.1G
CHOLESTEROL 6MG SODIUM 62MG

CINNAMON CANDY PUNCH

1 cup water
½ cup sugar
¼ cup plus 2 tablespoons cinnamon decorator
    candies
2 (46-ounce) cans unsweetened pineapple
    juice, chilled
8 cups raspberry-flavored ginger ale, chilled
Fresh mint sprigs (optional)
Pineapple cubes (optional)

Combine first 3 ingredients in a small saucepan; bring to a boil. Reduce heat; simmer, uncovered, 5 minutes or until candies melt, stirring occasionally. Cool completely.
  Combine cinnamon mixture and juice in a large punch bowl; stir well. Add ginger ale; stir gently. Pour into glasses; if desired, garnish with mint sprigs and pineapple cubes. Serve immediately. Yield: 22 (1-cup) servings.

PER SERVING: 125 CALORIES (0% FROM FAT)
FAT 0.1G (SATURATED FAT 0.0G)
PROTEIN 0.4G CARBOHYDRATE 32.0G
CHOLESTEROL 0MG SODIUM 6MG

Cinnamon Candy Punch

CITRUS SPRITZER

3 (3- x ½-inch) strips orange rind
3 (3- x ½-inch) strips grapefruit rind
4 cups pineapple-orange juice
2 cups fresh pink grapefruit juice
2 cups sparkling mineral water, chilled
Orange rind curls (optional)
Grapefruit rind curls (optional)

Place citrus strips in a glass pitcher; crush slightly by gently pressing against pitcher with back of a spoon. Add juices; stir well. Cover and chill thoroughly. Just before serving, stir in mineral water. Serve over ice. If desired, garnish with orange and grapefruit rind curls. Yield: 8 (1-cup) servings.

PER SERVING: 91 CALORIES (2% FROM FAT)
FAT 0.2G (SATURATED FAT 0.0G)
PROTEIN 0.6G   CARBOHYDRATE 22.4G
CHOLESTEROL 0MG   SODIUM 13MG

Sparkling Cranberry Blush

ORANGE-LIME MARGARITAS

(pictured on page 36)

1 cup unsweetened orange juice
¼ cup plus 2 tablespoons tequila
¼ cup Triple Sec or other orange-flavored liqueur
2 tablespoons fresh lime juice
1 (6-ounce) can frozen limeade concentrate, undiluted
4¼ cups crushed ice
Lime rind curls (optional)
Orange rind curls (optional)

Combine first 5 ingredients, stirring until limeade concentrate dissolves. Pour mixture into container of an electric blender. Add ice; cover and process 5 seconds. Pour into glasses. If desired, garnish with lime and orange rind curls. Yield: 5 (1-cup) servings.

PER SERVING: 166 CALORIES (1% FROM FAT)
FAT 0.1G (SATURATED FAT 0.0G)
PROTEIN 0.4G   CARBOHYDRATE 26.1G
CHOLESTEROL 0MG   SODIUM 1MG

SPARKLING CRANBERRY BLUSH

3 cups cold water
2 (48-ounce) bottles cranberry juice cocktail, chilled
2 (6-ounce) cans frozen lemonade concentrate, thawed and undiluted
2 (750-milliliter) bottles brut champagne, chilled

Combine first 3 ingredients in a punch bowl, and stir well. Add champagne; stir gently. Serve immediately. Yield: 32 (¾-cup) servings.

Note: To make ahead, combine first 3 ingredients; cover and chill. Just before serving, add champagne, and stir gently.

PER SERVING: 104 CALORIES (0% FROM FAT)
FAT 0.1G (SATURATED FAT 0.0G)
PROTEIN 0.2G   CARBOHYDRATE 18.2G
CHOLESTEROL 0MG   SODIUM 6MG

Hot Artichoke Dip

1 (14-ounce) can artichoke hearts, drained
2 tablespoons grated Parmesan cheese
2 tablespoons low-fat sour cream
1 small clove garlic
1 teaspoon lemon juice
4 drops of hot sauce
¾ cup plain low-fat yogurt (at room temperature)
Paprika

Position knife blade in food processor bowl; add first 6 ingredients, and process until artichokes are finely chopped. Combine artichoke mixture and yogurt; stir well. Spoon into a 1-quart baking dish; sprinkle with paprika. Bake at 350° for 25 minutes. Serve with French bread or breadsticks. Yield: 2 cups.

Per Tablespoon: 10 Calories (27% from Fat)
Fat 0.3g (Saturated Fat 0.2g)
Protein 0.7g Carbohydrate 1.3g
Cholesterol 1mg Sodium 35mg

Red Bean Hummus with Pita Wedges

3 cloves garlic
1 (16-ounce) can red beans, drained
2 tablespoons fresh lime juice
2 teaspoons sesame oil
¼ teaspoon ground cumin
3 (6-inch) pita bread rounds

Position knife blade in food processor bowl. Drop garlic through food chute with processor running; process 3 seconds or until minced. Add beans and next 3 ingredients; process until smooth.

Separate each pita bread round into 2 rounds; cut each round into 8 wedges. Serve hummus with pita wedges. Yield: 24 appetizer servings.

Note: Each appetizer serving includes 1 tablespoon hummus and 2 pita wedges.

Per Serving: 47 Calories (11% from Fat)
Fat 0.6g (Saturated Fat 0.1g)
Protein 1.7g Carbohydrate 8.2g
Cholesterol 0mg Sodium 49mg

Roasted Pepper Dip

(pictured on page 36)

3 large sweet red peppers
8 sun-dried tomato halves (packed without oil)
¾ cup boiling water
2 tablespoons chopped fresh parsley
1 tablespoon lemon juice
¼ teaspoon salt
¼ teaspoon pepper
1 clove garlic, minced
4 ounces ⅓-less-fat cream cheese, cubed and softened
½ cup nonfat sour cream

Cut peppers in half lengthwise; remove and discard seeds and membranes. Place peppers, skin sides up, on a baking sheet; flatten with palm of hand. Broil peppers 5½ inches from heat (with electric oven door partially opened) 15 to 20 minutes or until charred. Place peppers in ice water until cool. Remove peppers from water; peel and discard skins. Coarsely chop peppers.

Combine tomato halves and boiling water in a small bowl; let stand 5 minutes. Drain.

Position knife blade in food processor bowl; add chopped roasted pepper, tomato halves, parsley, and next 4 ingredients. Process until smooth, stopping once to scrape down sides. Add cheese and sour cream; process until smooth, stopping once to scrape down sides. Transfer pepper mixture to a serving bowl. Serve with crisp breadsticks or fresh raw vegetables. Yield: 2½ cups.

Note: For an unusual serving container, cut top off 1 large sweet red pepper; scoop out and discard seeds and membrane. Spoon dip into pepper, and place on a serving plate.

Per Tablespoon: 14 Calories (45% from Fat)
Fat 0.7g (Saturated Fat 0.4g)
Protein 0.6g Carbohydrate 1.2g
Cholesterol 2mg Sodium 36mg

SPINACH-HAM DIP

3 (1-pound) unsliced round loaves French
　　bread or sourdough bread
1 (10-ounce) package frozen chopped spinach,
　　thawed and drained
½ cup nonfat sour cream
1 (8-ounce) block ⅓-less-fat cream cheese,
　　softened
1 (8-ounce) carton plain nonfat yogurt
½ teaspoon garlic powder
1¼ cups diced cooked ham
1 (2-ounce) jar diced pimiento, drained
2 tablespoons grated Parmesan cheese

Slice off top fourth of 2 loaves, using a large serrated knife. Hollow out bottom pieces, leaving a
1-inch-thick shell; reserve remaining bread. Place 2
bread bowls on a baking sheet, and bake at 375° for
10 minutes or until bread is dry. Cut remaining loaf
and all reserved bread into bite-size pieces; place
on a baking sheet, and bake at 375° for 10 minutes
or until dry.

Press spinach between paper towels to remove
excess moisture. Combine sour cream and next 3
ingredients in a bowl; beat at medium speed of an
electric mixer just until smooth. Stir in spinach,
ham, and pimiento. Spoon mixture evenly into
bread bowls, and sprinkle evenly with Parmesan
cheese. Bake at 375° for 30 minutes or until thoroughly heated. Serve warm with reserved bread.
Yield: 30 appetizer servings.

Note: Each appetizer serving includes 2 tablespoons dip and 1 ounce bread.

PER SERVING: 110 CALORIES (22% FROM FAT)
FAT 2.7G (SATURATED FAT 1.5G)
PROTEIN 5.2G CARBOHYDRATE 15.5G
CHOLESTEROL 9MG SODIUM 241MG

ROASTED SWEET POTATO DIP

3 cups peeled, chopped sweet potato (about 1
　　pound)
2½ cups chopped onion
1½ cups chopped carrot
1 tablespoon olive oil
¼ cup tahini (sesame seed paste)
¼ teaspoon salt
⅛ teaspoon pepper

Combine first 4 ingredients, and place on a 15-
x 10- x 1-inch jellyroll pan; bake at 350° for 1 hour
or until sweet potato is tender.

Position knife blade in a food processor bowl;
add sweet potato mixture, tahini, salt, and pepper,
and process until smooth. Serve with breadsticks,
if desired. Yield: 3 cups.

PER TABLESPOON: 24 CALORIES (38% FROM FAT)
FAT 1.0G (SATURATED FAT 0.1G)
PROTEIN 0.5G CARBOHYDRATE 3.4G
CHOLESTEROL 0MG SODIUM 16MG

Roasted Sweet Potato Dip

Shrimp-Chutney Spread

SHRIMP-CHUTNEY SPREAD

Buy cooked shrimp from the supermarket to decrease the preparation time.

3 cups water
1 pound unpeeled medium-size fresh shrimp
1 (8-ounce) tub light process cream cheese, softened
½ cup nonfat sour cream
¼ cup finely chopped green onions
¼ cup mango chutney
1 tablespoon curry powder
¼ teaspoon salt
⅛ teaspoon ground white pepper
1 clove garlic, minced
Green onion curls (optional)

Bring water to a boil in a large saucepan; add shrimp. Cook 3 to 5 minutes or until shrimp turn pink. Drain well; rinse with cold water. Chill shrimp. Peel, devein, and finely chop shrimp. (If desired, peel 1 shrimp, leaving tail intact; set aside for garnish.)

Combine cream cheese and next 7 ingredients in a bowl; beat at medium speed of an electric mixer until blended. Stir in chopped shrimp. Cover and chill. Serve with low-fat crackers and fresh raw vegetables. If desired, garnish with reserved shrimp and green onion curls. Yield: 2¾ cups.

PER TABLESPOON: 26 CALORIES (35% FROM FAT)
FAT 1.0G (SATURATED FAT 0.5G)
PROTEIN 2.3G CARBOHYDRATE 1.9G
CHOLESTEROL 17MG SODIUM 76MG

SMOKED TURKEY AND SUN-DRIED TOMATO PÂTÉ

1¼ cups sun-dried tomato halves (packed
      without oil)
1 cup hot water
1½ pounds smoked turkey breast, cubed
½ cup tub-style light process cream cheese
¼ cup chopped onion
3 tablespoons dry white wine
2 tablespoons nonfat sour cream
2 teaspoons Dijon mustard
1 teaspoon white wine Worcestershire sauce
¼ teaspoon paprika
¼ teaspoon ground white pepper
2 tablespoons chopped fresh parsley
Vegetable cooking spray
⅛ teaspoon paprika
Fresh parsley sprigs (optional)

Combine tomato halves and water in a small
bowl; cover and let stand 15 minutes. Drain; set
aside 1 tomato half. Coarsely chop remaining
tomato halves; set aside.

Position knife blade in food processor bowl. Add
turkey and next 8 ingredients; process until
smooth, scraping sides of processor bowl once.
Transfer mixture to a medium bowl; stir in
chopped tomato and chopped parsley. Spoon mixture into a 4-cup mold coated with cooking spray.
Cover and chill 8 hours.

Unmold pâté onto a serving platter. Sprinkle
with paprika. Cut remaining softened sun-dried
tomato half into thin strips, and arrange over pâté.
Garnish with parsley sprigs, if desired. Serve with
French baguette rounds. Yield: 4 cups.

PER TABLESPOON: 19 CALORIES (28% FROM FAT)
FAT 0.6G (SATURATED FAT 0.3G)
PROTEIN 2.4G   CARBOHYDRATE 1.0G
CHOLESTEROL 6MG   SODIUM 107MG

Smoked Turkey and Sun-Dried Tomato Pâté

SPICY CHICKEN BITES WITH CUCUMBER DIP

1 pound skinned, boned chicken breasts, cut
　 into 1-inch pieces
¼ cup minced onion
1 large clove garlic, minced
1 egg, lightly beaten
⅓ cup fine, dry breadcrumbs
1 teaspoon ground ginger
½ teaspoon salt
½ teaspoon ground cumin
½ teaspoon ground red pepper
½ teaspoon curry powder
¼ teaspoon black pepper
3 tablespoons all-purpose flour
2 teaspoons vegetable oil
¼ teaspoon paprika
Cucumber Dip

Position knife blade in food processor bowl; add half of chicken. Pulse 6 times or until chicken is coarsely chopped. Spoon into a large bowl; repeat procedure with remaining chicken. Add onion, garlic, and egg to chicken. Combine breadcrumbs and next 6 ingredients; add to chicken mixture, stirring well. Shape mixture into 40 (1-inch) balls.

Place flour in a bowl. Roll each chicken ball in flour; place in an 11- x 7- x 1½-inch microwave-safe dish. Microwave at MEDIUM-HIGH (70% power) 6 minutes, stirring every 2 minutes.

Combine oil and paprika in a large skillet; place over medium heat until hot. Add chicken balls; cook 10 minutes, stirring occasionally. Serve warm with 1½ teaspoons Cucumber Dip per appetizer. Yield: 40 appetizer servings.

Spicy Chicken Bites with Cucumber Dip

CUCUMBER DIP

1 cup peeled, seeded, and grated
    cucumber
1 cup plain low-fat yogurt
1 teaspoon dried dillweed
½ teaspoon lemon juice

Place cucumber on several layers of paper towels; cover with additional paper towels. Let stand 15 minutes, pressing down occasionally.

Combine cucumber, yogurt, dillweed, and lemon juice in a bowl. Cover mixture, and chill. Yield: 1⅓ cups.

PER SERVING: 27 CALORIES (20% FROM FAT)
FAT 0.6G (SATURATED FAT 0.2G)
PROTEIN 3.3G   CARBOHYDRATE 1.8G
CHOLESTEROL 12MG   SODIUM 49MG

TERIYAKI CHICKEN DRUMMETTES WITH PINEAPPLE SAUCE

24 chicken drummettes, skinned
⅓ cup sugar
⅓ cup water
⅓ cup low-sodium soy sauce
¼ cup unsweetened pineapple juice
1 tablespoon vegetable oil
1 teaspoon peeled, grated gingerroot
1 clove garlic, crushed
Vegetable cooking spray
Pineapple Sauce

Place chicken in a heavy-duty, zip-top plastic bag. Combine sugar and next 6 ingredients; pour over chicken. Seal; shake until chicken is coated. Marinate in refrigerator 8 hours, turning bag occasionally. Remove chicken from marinade. Place marinade in a small saucepan; bring to a boil. Remove from heat.

Place chicken on rack of a broiler pan coated with cooking spray. Bake at 350° for 50 minutes or until done, turning and basting occasionally with marinade. Serve warm with 1 tablespoon Pineapple Sauce per appetizer. Yield: 24 appetizer servings.

PINEAPPLE SAUCE

1 (8-ounce) can crushed pineapple in juice,
    undrained
¼ cup firmly packed brown sugar
¼ cup cider vinegar
2 tablespoons ketchup
2 teaspoons cornstarch

Combine all ingredients in a small saucepan. Cook over medium heat, stirring constantly, until thickened. Yield: 1½ cups.

PER SERVING: 70 CALORIES (22% FROM FAT)
FAT 1.7G (SATURATED FAT 0.4G)
PROTEIN 5.6G   CARBOHYDRATE 7.6G
CHOLESTEROL 18MG   SODIUM 120MG

SANTA FE CHICKEN QUESADILLAS

1¼ cups no-salt-added salsa, divided
1 cup chopped cooked chicken breast
2 tablespoons chopped fresh cilantro
1 teaspoon ground cumin
1 (4.5-ounce) can chopped green chiles,
    drained
6 (7-inch) flour tortillas
1 cup (4 ounces) shredded reduced-fat sharp
    Cheddar cheese
Vegetable cooking spray

Combine ½ cup salsa and next 4 ingredients. Spoon mixture evenly onto half of each tortilla. Sprinkle with cheese.

Coat a nonstick skillet with cooking spray; place over medium-high heat until hot. Add 1 tortilla; cook 1 minute. Fold in half; cook 30 seconds. Turn; cook other side 30 seconds. Repeat with remaining tortillas. Cut each into 4 wedges. Top each wedge with ½ tablespoon salsa. Yield: 2 dozen.

PER APPETIZER: 61 CALORIES (28% FROM FAT)
FAT 1.9G (SATURATED FAT 0.7G)
PROTEIN 4.6G   CARBOHYDRATE 6.3G
CHOLESTEROL 9MG   SODIUM 129MG

CRAB-ARTICHOKE TARTS

2 teaspoons all-purpose flour
⅛ teaspoon dried thyme
⅛ teaspoon pepper
1 (4-ounce) carton fat-free egg substitute
¼ cup bottled roasted sweet red pepper, chopped
1 (14-ounce) can artichoke hearts, drained and chopped
1 (6-ounce) can crabmeat, drained
Vegetable cooking spray
32 wonton wrappers
3 tablespoons grated Parmesan cheese
2 tablespoons freeze-dried chives
1 tablespoon margarine, melted

Combine first 4 ingredients; add roasted pepper, artichokes, and crabmeat, stirring well.

Coat 32 miniature muffin cups with cooking spray. Gently press 1 wonton wrapper into each muffin cup, allowing ends to extend above edges of cups. Spoon crabmeat mixture evenly into wonton wrapper cups; sprinkle with cheese and chives. Brush edges of wonton wrappers with margarine. Bake at 350° for 20 minutes or until crabmeat mixture is set and edges of wonton wrappers are lightly browned. Yield: 32 appetizers.

PER APPETIZER: 35 CALORIES (18% FROM FAT)
FAT 0.7G (SATURATED FAT 0.2G)
PROTEIN 2.2G CARBOHYDRATE 4.9G
CHOLESTEROL 5MG SODIUM 108MG

Crab-Artichoke Tarts

SHRIMP WITH SILKEN TOMATO VINAIGRETTE

4 quarts water
2 large lemons, sliced
60 unpeeled medium-size fresh shrimp (about 2 pounds)
2 cups no-salt-added tomato juice
½ cup clam juice
¼ cup champagne or white wine vinegar
1½ tablespoons extra-virgin olive oil
1 tablespoon plus 1 teaspoon anchovy paste
Dash of ground white pepper
2 cloves garlic, crushed
1 cup chopped green pepper
1 cup chopped sweet yellow pepper
1 cup finely chopped tomato

Combine 4 quarts water and lemon slices in a large saucepan; bring to a boil. Add unpeeled shrimp, and cook 3 to 5 minutes or until shrimp turn pink. Drain well. Rinse with cold water; peel and devein shrimp. Cover shrimp, and chill.

Combine tomato juice and next 6 ingredients; stir with a wire whisk until blended. Cover and chill. Combine peppers and tomato; stir well. Cover and chill.

To serve, spoon ¼ cup tomato juice mixture into each of 12 shallow bowls. Place 5 shrimp in each bowl, and top each serving with ¼ cup pepper mixture. Yield: 12 appetizer servings.

PER SERVING: 99 CALORIES (28% FROM FAT)
FAT 3.1G (SATURATED FAT 0.4G)
PROTEIN 12.8G CARBOHYDRATE 4.8G
CHOLESTEROL 86MG SODIUM 341MG

WHITE BEAN BRUSCHETTA

This recipe calls for a baguette, a crispy-crusted long, thin loaf of French bread. You can substitute a loaf of regular French bread instead.

24 (½-inch-thick) slices French baguette
Olive oil-flavored vegetable cooking spray
¼ cup plus 2 tablespoons sun-dried tomato
    halves (packed without oil)
¼ cup boiling water
¼ cup finely chopped plum tomato
¼ cup plus 2 tablespoons chopped ripe olives
½ teaspoon dried basil
1 clove garlic, minced
1 (15-ounce) can cannellini beans, drained and
    mashed
2 teaspoons lemon juice
Fresh basil sprigs (optional)

Lightly coat both sides of bread slices with cooking spray; arrange in a single layer on a baking sheet. Bake at 350° for 10 to 12 minutes or until lightly browned, turning once.

Combine sun-dried tomato halves and water in a small bowl; cover and let stand 15 minutes. Drain and finely chop tomato halves. Combine sun-dried tomato, plum tomato, and next 3 ingredients. Cover and let stand 1 hour.

Combine beans and lemon juice; spread evenly over bread slices. Broil 5½ inches from heat (with electric oven door partially opened) 1 to 1½ minutes or until thoroughly heated. Spoon tomato mixture evenly over bean mixture. Garnish with fresh basil sprigs, if desired. Serve immediately. Yield: 2 dozen.

PER APPETIZER: 40 CALORIES (23% FROM FAT)
FAT 1.0G (SATURATED FAT 0.2G)
PROTEIN 1.4G CARBOHYDRATE 6.4G
CHOLESTEROL 0MG SODIUM 93MG

ARTICHOKE AND RED PEPPER PIZZA

1 (10-ounce) can refrigerated pizza dough
Vegetable cooking spray
1 tablespoon olive oil
1 cup julienne-sliced sweet red pepper
1 teaspoon dried basil
1 teaspoon dried oregano
5 cloves garlic, minced
1 (14-ounce) can artichoke hearts, drained and
    coarsely chopped
1 (2.5-ounce) jar sliced mushrooms, drained
1½ cups (6 ounces) shredded part-skim
    mozzarella cheese
Cracked pepper (optional)

Unroll pizza dough onto a baking sheet coated with cooking spray; pat dough into a 14- x 10-inch rectangle. Bake at 425° for 5 minutes; set aside.

Heat oil in a nonstick skillet over medium-high heat. Add red pepper and next 3 ingredients; sauté 5 minutes. Remove from heat; stir in artichokes and mushrooms.

Sprinkle half of cheese over prepared pizza crust, leaving a ½-inch border. Spread vegetable mixture evenly over cheese, and top with remaining cheese. Sprinkle with cracked pepper, if desired. Bake at 425° for 10 minutes or until crust is lightly browned. Yield: 16 appetizers.

PER APPETIZER: 101 CALORIES (32% FROM FAT)
FAT 3.6G (SATURATED FAT 1.3G)
PROTEIN 4.8G CARBOHYDRATE 12.7G
CHOLESTEROL 6MG SODIUM 256MG

Dresdner Stollen (recipe on page 65)

FROM THE BREAD BASKET

To fill your home with holiday spirit, just bake a loaf of bread. Its enticing aroma is guaranteed to create a feeling of hospitality.

Start out with one of several quick breads. Whether you make a simple biscuit, muffin, or loaf, you can stir these breads up quickly. Be sure to try Spiced Baked Doughnuts (page 54) for the children in the house—it's an easy, low-fat version that you bake instead of fry.

For a touch of old-world flavor, you can't beat St. Lucia Saffron Bread (page 66), Mocha Babka (page 63), or Dresdner Stollen (pictured at left). These yeast breads require a little extra time, but they're worth the effort for the tradition and the taste.

Unless otherwise indicated, bake bread in shiny aluminum pans. If you're using a glass dish or dark metal pan, decrease the oven temperature by 25 degrees, and bake the bread the same length of time.

Cheddar-Black Pepper Biscuits

CHEDDAR-BLACK PEPPER BISCUITS

2 cups all-purpose flour
1½ teaspoons baking powder
¼ teaspoon salt
¼ teaspoon coarsely ground pepper
2 tablespoons chilled stick margarine, cut into
    small pieces
¾ cup (3 ounces) shredded extra-sharp
    Cheddar cheese
¾ cup fat-free milk
Vegetable cooking spray
1 egg white, lightly beaten
¼ teaspoon coarsely ground pepper

Combine first 4 ingredients in a large bowl; cut in margarine with a pastry blender until mixture resembles coarse meal. Add cheese; toss well. Add milk, stirring just until dry ingredients are moistened.

Turn dough out onto a well-floured surface; knead 4 or 5 times. Roll dough to ½-inch thickness; cut into rounds with a 2-inch biscuit cutter.

Place rounds, 1 inch apart, on baking sheets coated with cooking spray, and brush with egg white; sprinkle with ¼ teaspoon pepper. Bake at 425° for 15 minutes or until lightly browned. Yield: 1½ dozen.

PER BISCUIT: 86 CALORIES (31% FROM FAT)
FAT 3.0G (SATURATED FAT 1.3G)
PROTEIN 3.2G   CARBOHYDRATE 11.3G
CHOLESTEROL 5MG   SODIUM 118MG

CRANBERRY SILVER DOLLAR BISCUITS

¼ cup warm water (105° to 115°)
1 package active dry yeast
2 cups all-purpose flour
1 teaspoon baking powder
½ teaspoon baking soda
¼ teaspoon salt
¼ cup sugar
3 tablespoons chilled stick margarine, cut into small pieces
¼ cup dried cranberries
¾ cup nonfat buttermilk
3 tablespoons all-purpose flour
Vegetable cooking spray

Combine warm water and yeast in a 1-cup liquid measuring cup; let stand 5 minutes.

Combine 2 cups flour and next 4 ingredients in a large bowl; cut in margarine with a pastry blender until mixture resembles coarse meal. Stir in cranberries. Add yeast mixture and buttermilk to flour mixture; stir with a fork just until dry ingredients are moistened.

Sprinkle 3 tablespoons flour evenly over work surface. Turn dough out onto floured surface; knead 4 or 5 times. Pat dough to ½-inch thickness; cut into rounds with a 1½-inch biscuit cutter. Place rounds on a baking sheet coated with cooking spray. Bake at 400° for 10 minutes or until biscuits are golden. Yield: 1½ dozen.

PER BISCUIT: 94 CALORIES (20% FROM FAT)
FAT 2.1G (SATURATED FAT 0.4G)
PROTEIN 2.2G   CARBOHYDRATE 16.6G
CHOLESTEROL 0MG   SODIUM 123MG

DATE AND MAPLE SCONES

2 cups all-purpose flour
1½ teaspoons baking powder
½ teaspoon baking soda
¼ teaspoon salt
¼ cup firmly packed brown sugar
⅓ cup chilled stick margarine, cut into small pieces
½ cup chopped pitted dates
½ cup low-fat milk
3 tablespoons maple syrup
Vegetable cooking spray

Combine first 5 ingredients in a large bowl; cut in margarine with a pastry blender until mixture resembles coarse meal. Add dates; toss well. Combine milk and syrup. Add to flour mixture, stirring just until dry ingredients are moistened.

Turn dough out onto a lightly floured surface; knead 4 or 5 times. Pat dough into an 8-inch circle on a baking sheet coated with cooking spray. Cut dough into 12 wedges, cutting into, but not through, dough. Bake at 400° for 15 minutes or until golden. Serve warm. Yield: 1 dozen.

PER SCONE: 176 CALORIES (28% FROM FAT)
FAT 5.5G (SATURATED FAT 1.1G)
PROTEIN 2.7G   CARBOHYDRATE 29.8G
CHOLESTEROL 0MG   SODIUM 218MG

Date and Maple Scones

EASY POPOVERS

*If you don't have any popover pans, use
eight 6-ounce ovenproof custard cups.*

1 cup bread flour
1 cup low-fat milk
¾ cup fat-free egg substitute
1 tablespoon sugar
1 tablespoon vegetable oil
¼ teaspoon salt
Vegetable cooking spray

Position knife blade in food processor bowl; add
first 6 ingredients. Process until smooth, stopping
once to scrape down sides.

Pour batter into popover pans coated with cooking spray, filling half full. Place in a cold oven. Turn
oven on 450°, and bake 15 minutes. Reduce oven
temperature to 350° (do not remove pans from
oven); bake 35 to 40 additional minutes or until
popovers are crusty and brown. Yield: 8 popovers.

PER POPOVER: 109 CALORIES (21% FROM FAT)
FAT 2.5G (SATURATED FAT 0.6G)
PROTEIN 5.3G CARBOHYDRATE 15.9G
CHOLESTEROL 1MG SODIUM 123MG

ORANGE POPOVERS

Add 2 teaspoons grated orange rind and 1 tablespoon unsweetened orange juice to flour mixture.
Proceed with recipe as directed.

PER POPOVER: 110 CALORIES (20% FROM FAT)
FAT 2.5G (SATURATED FAT 0.6G)
PROTEIN 5.3G CARBOHYDRATE 16.1G
CHOLESTEROL 1MG SODIUM 123MG

SAVORY DILLWEED POPOVERS

Add ½ teaspoon dried dillweed and ⅛ teaspoon
onion powder to flour mixture. Proceed with recipe
as directed.

PER POPOVER: 109 CALORIES (21% FROM FAT)
FAT 2.5G (SATURATED FAT 0.6G)
PROTEIN 5.3G CARBOHYDRATE 15.9G
CHOLESTEROL 1MG SODIUM 123MG

SPICED BAKED DOUGHNUTS

*In this recipe, a minibundt pan, which
looks like a muffin pan with six individual
cups, doubles as a doughnut mold.*

1½ cups all-purpose flour
1½ teaspoons baking powder
¼ teaspoon salt
½ cup plus 1 tablespoon sugar
1 teaspoon ground cinnamon
½ teaspoon ground nutmeg
½ cup low-fat milk
¼ cup stick margarine, melted
¼ cup fat-free egg substitute
½ teaspoon vanilla extract
Vegetable cooking spray
2 tablespoons powdered sugar

Combine first 6 ingredients in a large bowl; make
a well in center of mixture. Combine milk and next
3 ingredients; stir well. Add to dry ingredients, stirring just until moistened.

Spoon batter by 2 heaping tablespoonfuls into
each cup of a minibundt pan coated with cooking
spray. Smooth tops of batter evenly with a knife.
Bake at 400° for 12 minutes or until a wooden pick
inserted in center comes out clean. Remove from
pan immediately; cool on a wire rack. Repeat procedure with remaining batter. Sift powdered sugar
over doughnuts. Serve warm or at room temperature. Yield: 11 doughnuts.

Note: To make doughnut holes, spoon batter
evenly into 22 miniature muffin cups coated with
cooking spray. Bake at 400° for 10 minutes.

PER DOUGHNUT: 154 CALORIES (26% FROM FAT)
FAT 4.5G (SATURATED FAT 1.0G)
PROTEIN 2.7G CARBOHYDRATE 25.6G
CHOLESTEROL 0MG SODIUM 157MG

Spiced Baked Doughnuts

Cranberry-Citrus Muffins

CRANBERRY-CITRUS MUFFINS

2½ cups all-purpose flour
1 tablespoon baking powder
1 teaspoon baking soda
½ teaspoon salt
1½ cups fresh or frozen cranberries, thawed
1 cup sugar
2 egg whites, lightly beaten
1 egg, lightly beaten
¾ cup reduced-fat milk
⅓ cup light ricotta cheese
1 tablespoon grated orange rind
½ cup unsweetened orange juice
1 tablespoon grated lemon rind
2 tablespoons vegetable oil
1 tablespoon vanilla extract
Vegetable cooking spray
¼ cup plus 2 tablespoons turbinado or
   granulated sugar

Combine first 6 ingredients in a large bowl; make a well in center of mixture. Combine egg whites and next 8 ingredients; stir well with a wire whisk. Add to flour mixture, stirring just until dry ingredients are moistened.

Spoon batter evenly into muffin pans coated with cooking spray. Sprinkle turbinado sugar evenly over batter. Bake at 400° for 18 minutes or until done. Remove muffins from pans immediately. Yield: 1½ dozen.

PER MUFFIN: 159 CALORIES (14% FROM FAT)
FAT 2.4G (SATURATED FAT 0.6G)
PROTEIN 3.4G CARBOHYDRATE 31.4G
CHOLESTEROL 14MG SODIUM 220MG

MAPLE-SQUASH MUFFINS

1¾ cups all-purpose flour
1 teaspoon baking powder
½ teaspoon baking soda
⅛ teaspoon salt
1 teaspoon ground cinnamon
¼ cup finely chopped walnuts, toasted
2 egg whites, lightly beaten
¾ cup cooked, mashed butternut squash
⅔ cup plain nonfat yogurt
½ cup maple syrup
2 tablespoons vegetable oil
Vegetable cooking spray

Combine first 6 ingredients in a large bowl; make a well in center of mixture. Combine egg whites and next 4 ingredients; add to flour mixture, stirring just until dry ingredients are moistened.

Spoon batter evenly into muffin pans coated with cooking spray. Bake at 400° for 20 minutes. Remove from pans immediately. Yield: 1 dozen.

PER MUFFIN: 153 CALORIES (25% FROM FAT)
FAT 4.2G (SATURATED FAT 0.6G)
PROTEIN 3.9G CARBOHYDRATE 25.3G
CHOLESTEROL 0MG SODIUM 130MG

PEAR-WALNUT MUFFINS

A sprinkling of sugar on top gives these muffins a sweet, crispy crust.

1½ cups all-purpose flour
½ cup whole wheat flour or
    all-purpose flour
1 tablespoon baking powder
½ teaspoon salt
⅔ cup firmly packed brown sugar
½ teaspoon ground cinnamon
1¼ cups finely chopped pear
⅓ cup coarsely chopped walnuts, toasted
1 egg, lightly beaten
¾ cup reduced-fat milk
2 tablespoons vegetable oil
Vegetable cooking spray
1 tablespoon sugar

Combine first 6 ingredients in a large bowl; add pear and walnuts, tossing gently to coat. Make a well in center of mixture. Combine egg, milk, and oil. Add to flour mixture, stirring just until dry ingredients are moistened (dough will be sticky).

Spoon batter evenly into muffin pans coated with cooking spray; sprinkle with 1 tablespoon sugar. Bake at 400° for 20 minutes or until a wooden pick inserted in center comes out clean. Remove muffins from pans immediately. Yield: 1 dozen.

PER MUFFIN: 175 CALORIES (27% FROM FAT)
FAT 5.3G (SATURATED FAT 0.9G)
PROTEIN 4.3G   CARBOHYDRATE 28.6G
CHOLESTEROL 20MG   SODIUM 215MG

Pear-Walnut Muffins

CARDAMOM COFFEE CAKE

¼ cup chopped walnuts
2 tablespoons all-purpose flour
2 tablespoons sugar
1 teaspoon ground cinnamon
1 tablespoon chilled stick margarine, cut
  into small pieces
1 cup all-purpose flour
½ teaspoon baking powder
¼ teaspoon baking soda
⅛ teaspoon salt
⅓ cup sugar
¼ teaspoon ground cardamom
1 egg, lightly beaten
½ cup plain low-fat yogurt
1½ tablespoons margarine, melted
Vegetable cooking spray
2 teaspoons all-purpose flour
1 medium Bosc pear (about ½ pound),
  peeled, cored, and cut into ¼-inch
  wedges

Combine first 4 ingredients in a bowl; cut in 1 tablespoon margarine with a pastry blender until mixture resembles coarse meal. Set aside.

Combine 1 cup flour and next 5 ingredients in a large bowl; stir well. Combine egg, yogurt, and melted margarine; stir well. Add to flour mixture, stirring just until dry ingredients are moistened.

Coat a 9-inch round cakepan with cooking spray; lightly dust with 2 teaspoons flour. Spread batter into prepared pan. Arrange pear wedges over batter, spoke-fashion, around edge of pan, overlapping slightly (do not place pears over center of batter).

Sprinkle walnut mixture evenly over coffee cake. Bake at 350° for 30 minutes or until a wooden pick inserted in center comes out clean. To serve, cut into wedges. Serve warm. Yield: 8 wedges.

PER WEDGE: 198 CALORIES (32% FROM FAT)
FAT 7.0G (SATURATED FAT 1.2G)
PROTEIN 4.4G CARBOHYDRATE 30.4G
CHOLESTEROL 27MG SODIUM 122MG

Cardamom Coffee Cake

RUM-APPLE BREAD

¼ cup stick margarine, softened
1 cup firmly packed brown sugar
½ cup fat-free egg substitute
¼ cup dark rum
1¾ cups all-purpose flour
1 teaspoon baking powder
½ teaspoon baking soda
½ teaspoon salt
1 cup peeled, coarsely shredded Granny Smith
    apple
½ cup raisins
¼ cup chopped walnuts
Vegetable cooking spray

Beat margarine in a large bowl at medium speed of an electric mixer; gradually add sugar, beating at medium speed until light and fluffy (about 5 minutes). Add egg substitute, and beat until well blended. Add rum; beat well.

Combine flour and next 3 ingredients. Add to margarine mixture; beat well. Stir in apple, raisins, and walnuts.

Pour batter into a 9- x 5- x 3-inch loafpan coated with cooking spray. Bake at 350° for 1 hour or until a wooden pick inserted in center comes out clean. Cool in pan on a wire rack 10 minutes; remove from pan, and cool completely on wire rack. Yield: 1 loaf, 18 (½-inch) slices.

PER SLICE: 131 CALORIES (25% FROM FAT)
FAT 3.6G (SATURATED FAT 0.6G)
PROTEIN 2.4G CARBOHYDRATE 20.9G
CHOLESTEROL 0MG SODIUM 154MG

MOM'S BANANA BREAD

1 cup sugar
¼ cup light butter, softened
1⅔ cups mashed ripe banana
¼ cup fat-free milk
¼ cup low-fat sour cream
2 egg whites
2 cups all-purpose flour
1 teaspoon baking soda
½ teaspoon salt
Vegetable cooking spray

Combine sugar and butter in a large bowl; beat at medium speed of an electric mixer until well blended. Add banana and next 3 ingredients; beat well. Combine flour, soda, and salt, stirring well; add to banana mixture, beating until blended.

Spoon batter into four 5- x 2½-inch miniature loafpans coated with cooking spray. Bake at 350° for 45 minutes or until a wooden pick inserted in center comes out clean. Cool in pans on wire racks 10 minutes; remove from pans. Cool completely on wire racks. Yield: 4 loaves, 4 slices each.

Note: To make one 9-inch loaf, spoon batter into a 9- x 5- x 3-inch loafpan coated with cooking spray; bake at 350° for 1 hour and 10 minutes. Yield: 1 loaf, 18 (½-inch) slices.

PER SLICE: 147 CALORIES (14% FROM FAT)
FAT 2.2G (SATURATED FAT 1.4G)
PROTEIN 2.5G CARBOHYDRATE 30.2G
CHOLESTEROL 7MG SODIUM 180MG

Give a Gift of Bread

As the holiday season begins, take a few minutes to bake some loaves of quick bread with the recipes on this and the following pages. They take little effort to put together, and they freeze beautifully. You'll be able to take one out of the freezer every time you think of someone who needs a gift.

Cool freshly baked bread completely before wrapping it. Wrap it first in plastic wrap; then overwrap it in aluminum foil before freezing or in decorative wrapping for immediate gift-giving. Seal tightly to prevent the bread from drying out. You can freeze these breads successfully up to one month.

GRAPEFRUIT-PECAN BREAD

1 large pink grapefruit (about 1¼ pounds)
2 cups all-purpose flour
¾ teaspoon baking soda
½ teaspoon baking powder
¼ teaspoon salt
¾ cup sugar
1 egg, lightly beaten
2 tablespoons vegetable oil
1 teaspoon vanilla extract
½ cup chopped pecans
Vegetable cooking spray
½ cup sifted powdered sugar
1 tablespoon water

Grate 1 tablespoon grapefruit rind; set aside grated rind. Peel and section grapefruit over a bowl, reserving juice and membranes. Set sections aside.

Squeeze membranes to extract juice; discard membranes. Position knife blade in food processor bowl; add grapefruit sections and juice, and pulse 3 times. Set aside 1¼ cups mixture; reserve remaining grapefruit mixture for another use.

Combine grapefruit rind, flour, and next 4 ingredients in a large bowl; make a well in center of mixture.

Combine egg, oil, vanilla, and reserved 1¼ cups grapefruit mixture; stir well. Add to flour mixture, stirring just until dry ingredients are moistened. Stir in pecans.

Pour batter into an 8½- x 4½- x 3-inch loafpan coated with cooking spray. Bake at 350° for 1 hour or until a wooden pick inserted in center comes out clean. Remove from oven, and place in pan on a wire rack.

Combine powdered sugar and water; stir well with a wire whisk. Drizzle over bread; cool in pan 10 minutes. Remove from pan; cool completely on wire rack. Yield: 1 loaf, 16 (½-inch) slices.

PER SLICE: 156 CALORIES (27% FROM FAT)
FAT 4.7G (SATURATED FAT 0.6G)
PROTEIN 2.3G CARBOHYDRATE 26.8G
CHOLESTEROL 14MG SODIUM 93MG

PEAR AND POPPY SEED LOAF

2¼ cups all-purpose flour
1½ teaspoons baking powder
1 teaspoon baking soda
½ teaspoon salt
3 tablespoons poppy seeds
⅛ teaspoon ground cardamom
1 cup peeled, chopped ripe pear
1 egg, lightly beaten
1 cup low-fat buttermilk
⅔ cup sugar
¼ cup honey
2 tablespoons stick margarine, melted
1 teaspoon vanilla extract
Vegetable cooking spray

Combine first 6 ingredients in a large bowl. Stir in pear; make a well in center of mixture. Combine egg and next 5 ingredients; stir well with a wire whisk. Add to flour mixture, stirring just until dry ingredients are moistened.

Pour batter into an 8½- x 4½- x 3-inch loafpan coated with cooking spray. Bake at 350° for 1 hour and 5 minutes or until a wooden pick inserted in center comes out clean. Cool in pan on a wire rack 10 minutes; remove from pan. Cool completely on wire rack. Yield: 1 loaf, 16 (½-inch) slices.

PER SLICE: 151 CALORIES (17% FROM FAT)
FAT 2.8G (SATURATED FAT 0.5G)
PROTEIN 3.2G CARBOHYDRATE 29.0G
CHOLESTEROL 14MG SODIUM 228MG

Pear and Poppy Seed Loaf

Mocha Babka (left) and Maple-Oat Bread with Prune Filling

MAPLE-OAT BREAD WITH PRUNE FILLING

1½ cups regular oats, uncooked
½ cup oat bran
2 packages active dry yeast
¼ teaspoon sugar
1⅓ cups warm water (105° to 115°), divided
¼ cup low-fat buttermilk powder
1 teaspoon salt
1 teaspoon ground cardamom
½ cup maple syrup
⅓ cup vegetable oil
2 egg whites, lightly beaten
4 to 4¼ cups bread flour, divided
Vegetable cooking spray
1 cup pitted prunes
1 tablespoon brandy
½ cup sifted powdered sugar
2 teaspoons water
½ teaspoon vanilla extract

Combine oats and bran in container of an electric blender or food processor; cover and process until mixture resembles fine meal. Set aside.

Combine yeast, sugar, and ⅔ cup warm water; let stand 10 minutes. Combine remaining ⅔ cup warm water, buttermilk powder, and next 5 ingredients in a large bowl; stir well. Add oats mixture, yeast mixture, and ½ cup bread flour; beat at high speed of an electric mixer 2 minutes. Stir in 3 cups bread flour, ½ cup at a time, to make a stiff dough.

Turn dough out onto a lightly floured surface. Knead until smooth and elastic (about 8 minutes); add enough of remaining flour, 1 tablespoon at a time, to keep dough from sticking to hands. Place dough in a bowl coated with cooking spray, turning to coat top. Cover and let rise in a warm place (85°), free from drafts, 1 hour or until doubled in bulk.

Place prunes in a small saucepan; add water to cover. Bring to a boil; reduce heat. Simmer, uncovered, 15 minutes or until softened. Drain. Combine prunes and brandy in container of an electric blender; cover and process until smooth. Set aside.

Punch dough down, and turn out onto a lightly floured surface; knead 4 or 5 times. Divide dough in half; roll each half into a 15- x 9-inch rectangle. Place on a baking sheet coated with cooking spray. Spoon half of prune mixture lengthwise down center third of dough. Make diagonal cuts, 1½ inches apart, on opposite sides of filling to within ½ inch of filling. Fold strips alternately over filling from each side, overlapping at an angle. Repeat procedure with remaining dough and prune mixture. Cover and let rise in a warm place, free from drafts, 50 minutes or until doubled in bulk.

Bake at 350° for 30 minutes or until golden. Cool on wire racks. Combine powdered sugar, 2 teaspoons water, and vanilla; stir well. Drizzle over loaves. Yield: 2 loaves, 16 (1-inch) slices each.

PER SLICE: 137 CALORIES (20% FROM FAT)
FAT 3.1G (SATURATED FAT 0.5G)
PROTEIN 3.6G CARBOHYDRATE 23.7G
CHOLESTEROL 0MG SODIUM 82MG

MOCHA BABKA

4½ to 4¾ cups bread flour, divided
¾ cup medium rye flour
⅓ cup firmly packed brown sugar
¼ cup instant nonfat dry milk powder
1 teaspoon instant coffee granules
¾ teaspoon salt
2 packages active dry yeast
1¼ cups water
½ cup semisweet chocolate morsels
¼ cup plus 2 tablespoons reduced-calorie
   stick margarine
4 egg whites
2 tablespoons bread flour
Vegetable cooking spray
Chocolate Streusel

Combine 1 cup bread flour and next 6 ingredients in a large bowl; stir well. Combine water,

chocolate, and margarine in a small saucepan; cook over medium heat, stirring constantly, until chocolate and margarine melt. Cool to 120° to 130°.

Add chocolate mixture to flour mixture; beat at low speed of an electric mixer 1 minute. Add egg whites; beat at medium-high 1 minute. Stir in enough of remaining bread flour to make a soft dough.

Sprinkle 2 tablespoons bread flour over work surface. Turn dough out onto surface; knead until smooth and elastic (about 8 minutes). Place dough in a bowl coated with cooking spray, turning to coat top. Cover and let rise in a warm place (85°), free from drafts, 55 minutes or until doubled in bulk.

Punch dough down; turn out onto floured surface, and knead 4 or 5 times. Divide dough in half. Roll 1 portion into a 12- x 8-inch rectangle. Sprinkle half of Chocolate Streusel over rectangle, leaving a 1-inch margin around edges.

Roll up dough, starting at long side, pressing firmly to eliminate air pockets; pinch long edge to seal. Place dough, seam side down, in a 10-cup tube pan coated with cooking spray; pinch ends together. Repeat procedure with remaining dough and Chocolate Streusel; place, seam side down, on roll in tube pan. Cover; let rise in a warm place, free from drafts, 45 minutes or until doubled in bulk. Bake at 350° for 40 minutes or until loaf sounds hollow when tapped. (Cover loaf with foil last 10 minutes of baking to prevent excessive browning, if necessary.) Let stand 10 minutes. Remove from pan; cool. Yield: 1 loaf, 28 (1-inch) slices.

CHOCOLATE STREUSEL
½ cup firmly packed dark brown sugar
¼ cup bread flour
2 tablespoons unsweetened cocoa
½ teaspoon ground cinnamon
3 tablespoons chilled reduced-calorie stick
   margarine, cut into small pieces

Position knife blade in food processor bowl; add first 4 ingredients. Process until combined. Add margarine; pulse 5 times or until mixture resembles coarse meal. Yield: 1 cup.

PER SLICE: 167 CALORIES (22% FROM FAT)
FAT 4.1G (SATURATED FAT 1.1G)
PROTEIN 4.4G CARBOHYDRATE 28.8G
CHOLESTEROL 0MG SODIUM 115MG

SOURDOUGH STARTER

2 cups all-purpose flour
¼ cup sugar, divided
1 teaspoon salt
1 package active dry yeast
2 cups warm water (105° to 115°)

Combine flour, 3 tablespoons sugar, and salt in a bowl; stir well, and set aside.

Dissolve yeast and remaining 1 tablespoon sugar in warm water in a medium nonmetallic bowl; let stand 5 minutes. Add flour mixture, stirring with a wire whisk until blended. Pour into a 2-quart glass jar or ceramic container; cover with cheesecloth, a cotton towel, or vented plastic wrap. Let stand in a warm place (85°) for 3 days, stirring once daily. Refrigerate 7 days, stirring once daily.

Remove Sourdough Starter from refrigerator; stir well, and set aside the amount needed for Sourdough Bread (recipe at right), or discard 1 cup. Let stand at room temperature 3 hours. Feed remaining Sourdough Starter with Starter Food (recipe below), and let stand at room temperature 24 hours. Refrigerate 7 days, stirring once daily. Yield: 4 (1-cup) servings.

Note: Every 7 days remove at least 1 cup Sourdough Starter to give away, use in recipe, or discard; leave at least 1 cup starter to continue cycle. When alive, the starter has a pleasant yeasty smell, is visibly bubbly, and is thick when stirred. When dead, the starter has a pungent vinegary smell, has no visible bubbles, and is thin and watery; it should be discarded.

STARTER FOOD

"Feed" your Sourdough Starter with this mixture every 7 days.

1 cup all-purpose flour
½ cup sugar
1 cup water

Combine all ingredients; stir well. Yield: 1¾ cups.

PER SERVING: 281 CALORIES (2% FROM FAT)
FAT 0.7G (SATURATED FAT 0.1G)
PROTEIN 7.1G CARBOHYDRATE 60.8G
CHOLESTEROL 0MG SODIUM 587MG

Sourdough Bread

SOURDOUGH BREAD

1 package active dry yeast
½ cup sugar, divided
1½ cups warm water (105° to 115°)
1½ cups Sourdough Starter
½ cup vegetable oil
2 teaspoons salt
8 to 8½ cups all-purpose flour, divided
Vegetable cooking spray

Combine yeast, 2 tablespoons sugar, and water in a large bowl; let stand 5 minutes. Add remaining sugar, Sourdough Starter (at room temperature), oil, and salt; stir well. Add 2 cups flour, stirring until well blended; stir in 6 cups flour to make a soft dough. Turn dough out onto a lightly floured surface. Knead until smooth and elastic (about 12 minutes); add enough of remaining flour, 1 tablespoon at a time, to keep dough from sticking to hands.

Place dough in a large bowl coated with cooking spray, turning to coat top. Cover and let rise in a warm place (85°), free from drafts, 1½ hours or until doubled in bulk. Punch dough down; turn out onto a lightly floured surface. Divide dough in half; roll each portion into a 14- x 8-inch rectangle. Roll up rectangles, starting at short ends, pressing firmly to eliminate air pockets; pinch edges to seal. Place each roll, seam side down, in a 9- x 5- x 3-inch loafpan coated with cooking spray. Cover; let rise in a warm place, free from drafts, 1½ hours or until doubled in bulk.

Uncover; bake at 350° for 35 minutes or until loaves sound hollow when tapped. Remove from pans; cool on wire racks. Yield: 2 loaves, 18 slices each.

PER SLICE: 151 CALORIES (20% FROM FAT)
FAT 3.4G (SATURATED FAT 0.6G)
PROTEIN 3.2G CARBOHYDRATE 26.6G
CHOLESTEROL 0MG SODIUM 155MG

DRESDNER STOLLEN

(pictured on page 50)

¼ cup candied orange peel
¼ cup coarsely chopped red candied
   cherries
¼ cup currants
¼ cup golden raisins
2 tablespoons brandy
1 tablespoon vanilla extract
½ cup low-fat milk
¼ cup sugar
2 tablespoons stick margarine
1 package active dry yeast
1 teaspoon sugar
2 tablespoons warm water (105° to 115°)
2½ to 3 cups all-purpose flour, divided
1 teaspoon grated lemon rind
½ teaspoon ground nutmeg
1 egg
½ cup slivered almonds, toasted
Vegetable cooking spray
2 teaspoons sugar, divided
½ cup sifted powdered sugar
2 teaspoons low-fat milk

Combine first 6 ingredients in a small bowl; let stand 2 hours, stirring occasionally. Drain; set fruit mixture aside.

Heat ½ cup milk over medium-high heat in a heavy saucepan to 180° or until tiny bubbles form around edge. (Do not boil.) Remove from heat; add ¼ cup sugar and margarine, stirring until margarine melts. Cool.

Combine yeast, 1 teaspoon sugar, and 2 tablespoons warm water in a bowl; let stand 5 minutes. Add milk mixture, 1 cup flour, and next 3 ingredients. Beat at low speed of an electric mixer 2 minutes or until smooth. Stir in 1 cup flour, ½ cup at a time, to make a soft dough.

Turn dough out onto a lightly floured surface. Knead until smooth and elastic (about 8 minutes); add enough remaining flour, 1 tablespoon at a time, to keep dough from sticking to hands.

Combine fruit mixture, almonds, and 1 tablespoon flour; stir well. Add to dough in 2 batches, kneading until all fruit is combined; add enough remaining flour, 1 tablespoon at a time, to keep dough from sticking to hands.

Place dough in a large bowl coated with cooking spray, turning to coat top. Cover and let rise in a warm place (85°), free from drafts, 1 hour or until doubled in bulk.

Punch dough down; let rest 5 minutes. Turn out onto a lightly floured surface; roll into a 12- x 8-inch rectangle. Sprinkle 1½ teaspoons sugar over entire surface. Fold dough in half lengthwise, leaving a ½-inch margin; pinch seam to seal. Sprinkle with remaining ½ teaspoon sugar. Place dough, seam side up, on a baking sheet coated with cooking spray. Cover; let rise in a warm place, free from drafts, 30 minutes or until doubled in bulk.

Bake at 350° for 20 minutes. Reduce oven temperature to 300° (do not remove pan from oven); bake 15 minutes or until loaf sounds hollow when tapped. Cool on wire rack. Combine powdered sugar and 2 teaspoons milk; stir well. Drizzle over loaf. Yield: 1 loaf, 26 (½-inch) slices.

PER SLICE: 106 CALORIES (20% FROM FAT)
FAT 2.3G (SATURATED FAT 0.4G)
PROTEIN 2.3G CARBOHYDRATE 18.7G
CHOLESTEROL 9MG SODIUM 17MG

CINNAMON-RAISIN BREAD

¼ cup sugar
1 package active dry yeast
1 cup warm fat-free milk (105° to 115°)
3¾ cups all-purpose flour, divided
2 tablespoons vegetable oil
1 teaspoon salt
1 egg, lightly beaten
½ cup raisins
Vegetable cooking spray
1 tablespoon vegetable oil
¼ cup sugar
1 teaspoon ground cinnamon

Combine first 3 ingredients in a large bowl. Let stand 5 minutes. Add 1½ cups flour and next 3 ingredients; beat at medium speed of an electric mixer until smooth. Add 2 cups flour and raisins, stirring to make a soft dough.

Turn dough out onto a lightly floured surface. Knead until smooth and elastic (about 5 minutes); add enough of remaining ¼ cup flour, 1 tablespoon at a time, to keep dough from sticking to hands. Place dough in a bowl coated with cooking spray, turning to coat top. Cover and let rise in a warm place (85°), free from drafts, 1 hour or until doubled in bulk.

Punch dough down, and turn out onto a lightly floured surface; roll into a 15- x 9-inch rectangle. Brush 1 tablespoon oil over dough. Combine ¼ cup sugar and cinnamon, and sprinkle over dough, leaving a ½-inch margin around edges. Roll up tightly, starting at short side, pressing firmly to eliminate air pockets; pinch seam and edges to seal. Place roll, seam side down, in a 9- x 5- x 3-inch loafpan coated with cooking spray. Cover and let rise in a warm place, free from drafts, 45 minutes or until doubled in bulk.

Uncover; bake at 350° for 40 minutes or until loaf sounds hollow when tapped. Remove from pan; cool on a wire rack. Yield: 1 loaf, 18 (½-inch) slices.

PER SLICE: 152 CALORIES (17% FROM FAT)
FAT 2.9G (SATURATED FAT 0.6G)
PROTEIN 3.6G   CARBOHYDRATE 28.0G
CHOLESTEROL 12MG   SODIUM 142MG

ST. LUCIA SAFFRON BREAD

2 packages active dry yeast
2 cups warm water (105° to 115°)
⅓ cup honey
⅛ teaspoon saffron powder
7 to 7½ cups all-purpose flour, divided
½ cup instant nonfat dry milk powder
¼ cup golden raisins
1 teaspoon salt
2 egg whites
1 egg
¼ cup stick margarine, melted
Vegetable cooking spray
2 tablespoons fat-free milk
1 egg white, lightly beaten
2 tablespoons sliced almonds
2 tablespoons coarsely crushed sugar cubes

Combine yeast and warm water in a large bowl. Add honey and saffron; let stand 5 minutes. Add 3 cups flour and next 5 ingredients; beat at medium speed of an electric mixer until smooth. Add margarine, beating until combined. Stir in 4 cups flour to make a soft dough.

Turn dough out onto a lightly floured surface. Knead until smooth and elastic (about 10 minutes); add enough remaining flour, 1 tablespoon at a time, to keep dough from sticking to hands.

Place dough in a large bowl coated with cooking spray, turning to coat top. Cover and let rise in a warm place (85°), free from drafts, 1 hour or until doubled in bulk.

Punch dough down; turn out onto a lightly floured surface. Divide into 3 equal portions, shaping each portion into a 36-inch rope. Place ropes lengthwise on a baking sheet covered with parchment paper. Braid ropes, starting from center and braiding to ends. Cut ends to even strands, reserving any remaining dough. Shape braid into a wreath, pinching ends together to seal. Shape reserved dough into a bow; place over seam of wreath. Cover; let rise in a warm place, free from drafts, 15 minutes. (Dough will not double in bulk.)

Uncover dough. Combine milk and 1 egg white; brush over dough. Sprinkle dough with almonds and sugar. Bake at 375° for 35 minutes or until golden. Cool on a wire rack. Yield: 1 loaf, 45 (1-inch) slices.

PER SLICE: 103 CALORIES (13% FROM FAT)
FAT 1.5G (SATURATED FAT 0.3G)
PROTEIN 3.1G CARBOHYDRATE 19.2G
CHOLESTEROL 5MG SODIUM 77MG

APPLE-FILLED SWEET ROLLS

1½ cups unsweetened applesauce
3 tablespoons brown sugar
1½ teaspoons apple pie spice, divided
1 tablespoon plus 1 teaspoon cornstarch
1 tablespoon plus ½ teaspoon vanilla extract, divided
1 package active dry yeast
⅓ cup warm water (105° to 115°)
3 tablespoons sugar
¾ teaspoon salt
1 egg, beaten
½ cup warm fat-free milk (105° to 115°)
3¼ cups all-purpose flour, divided
Vegetable cooking spray
¼ cup sifted powdered sugar
1½ teaspoons water

Combine applesauce, brown sugar, and ¾ teaspoon apple pie spice in a saucepan; cook over medium heat 20 minutes, stirring often. Combine cornstarch and 1 tablespoon vanilla; add to saucepan, stirring well. Cook 1 minute or until thickened; remove from heat, and cool.

Combine yeast and warm water in a bowl; let stand 5 minutes. Add remaining ¾ teaspoon apple pie spice, 3 tablespoons sugar, salt, and egg; stir well. Stir in milk. Gradually stir in 3 cups flour to make a stiff dough. Turn out onto a lightly floured surface; shape into a ball. Cover; let rest 5 minutes. Knead dough until smooth and elastic (about 10 minutes); add enough remaining flour to keep dough from sticking to hands.

Place dough in a large bowl coated with cooking spray, turning to coat top. Cover and let rise in a warm place (85°), free from drafts, 45 minutes or until doubled in bulk.

Punch dough down; divide in half. Turn out 1 dough portion onto a lightly floured surface; roll into a 12- x 9-inch rectangle. Spread half of applesauce mixture over entire surface, leaving a ½-inch margin along edges. Beginning at long edges, roll up dough, jellyroll fashion; pinch seam to seal. (Do not seal ends.) Repeat procedure with remaining dough and applesauce mixture. Cut each roll into 12 (1-inch) slices; arrange slices, cut side up, in a circle on baking sheets coated with cooking spray.

Cover and let rise in a warm place (85°), free from drafts, 45 minutes or until doubled in bulk. Bake at 375° for 20 minutes. Remove from baking sheet; place on a wire rack. Combine powdered sugar, 1½ teaspoons water, and remaining ½ teaspoon vanilla; brush over rolls. Yield: 2 dozen.

PER ROLL: 94 CALORIES (5% FROM FAT)
FAT 0.5G (SATURATED FAT 0.1G)
PROTEIN 2.3G CARBOHYDRATE 19.5G
CHOLESTEROL 9MG SODIUM 80MG

Apple-Filled Sweet Rolls

68

Creamy Lobster with Angel Hair Pasta (recipe on page 83)

ELEGANT ENTRÉES

Whether you're hosting a family reunion, a group from the office, or your neighborhood friends, you'll want exceptional entrées for holiday feasting. You can stick to tradition and serve a baked ham for Christmas dinner or brisket for Hanukkah. Or perhaps you want to try a new dish, such as Filet Mignon with Mushroom Wine Sauce (page 70) or Crawfish Fettuccine (page 81). Either way, you'll find the perfect recipe here—lightened but still rich in taste.

For a large gathering, consider one of the beef, pork, veal, or lamb roast recipes. Creamy Lobster with Angel Hair Pasta (page 83) and Grecian Cornish Hens (page 77) are impressive dishes for smaller, more intimate holiday parties.

You'll find plenty of elaborate recipes worthy of the holiday season. But this chapter also offers you a variety of quicker recipes. Italian Chicken Rolls (page 77), Holiday Turkey Cutlets (page 80), and Spicy Shrimp Creole (page 82) are three of the easiest.

FILET MIGNON WITH MUSHROOM-WINE SAUCE

1 tablespoon margarine, divided
Vegetable cooking spray
⅓ cup finely chopped shallot
½ pound fresh shiitake mushrooms, stems
    removed
1½ cups dry red wine, divided
1 (10½-ounce) can beef consommé,
    undiluted and divided
Cracked pepper
4 (4-ounce) filet mignon steaks
1 tablespoon low-sodium soy sauce
2 teaspoons cornstarch
1 tablespoon chopped fresh thyme
Fresh thyme sprigs (optional)

Melt 1½ teaspoons margarine in a nonstick skillet coated with cooking spray over medium heat. Add shallot and mushrooms; sauté 4 minutes. Add 1 cup wine and ¾ cup consommé; cook 5 minutes, stirring often. Remove mushrooms; place in a bowl. Increase heat to high; cook wine mixture 5 minutes or until reduced to ½ cup. Add to mushrooms; set aside. Wipe skillet with a paper towel.

Sprinkle cracked pepper over steaks. Melt remaining 1½ teaspoons margarine in skillet coated with cooking spray over medium heat. Add steaks; cook 3 minutes on each side or until browned. Reduce heat to medium-low; cook 1½ minutes on each side or to desired degree of doneness.

Combine soy sauce and cornstarch; stir well. Add remaining wine and consommé to skillet; scrape skillet to loosen browned bits. Bring to a boil; cook 1 minute. Add mushroom mixture, cornstarch mixture, and chopped thyme; bring to a boil. Cook, stirring constantly, 1 minute. Serve with steaks. Garnish with thyme sprigs, if desired. Yield: 4 servings.

PER SERVING: 250 CALORIES (39% FROM FAT)
FAT 10.7G (SATURATED FAT 3.6G)
PROTEIN 28.5G   CARBOHYDRATE 9.4G
CHOLESTEROL 84MG   SODIUM 712MG

Filet Mignon with Mushroom-Wine Sauce

Brisket with Vegetables

BRISKET WITH VEGETABLES

1 (2½-pound) beef brisket
1 teaspoon browning-and-seasoning sauce
2 cloves garlic, crushed
½ teaspoon salt
¼ teaspoon pepper
¾ teaspoon paprika
2 tablespoons all-purpose flour, divided
1 cup sliced onion, separated into rings
6 medium carrots, cut into 1½-inch pieces
12 small unpeeled round red potatoes
½ cup plus 2 tablespoons water, divided
½ cup dry red wine
1 (8-ounce) can no-salt-added tomato sauce

Trim fat from brisket; brush top with browning-and-seasoning sauce. Spread garlic over brisket; sprinkle with salt, pepper, and paprika. Set aside.

Sprinkle 1 tablespoon flour in an oven cooking bag. Arrange onion rings in bag, and place brisket over onion. Arrange carrot and potatoes around and on brisket.

Combine ½ cup water, wine, and tomato sauce; stir and add to bag. Seal bag; place in a 13- x 9- x 2-inch baking pan. Cut six ½-inch slits in top of bag.

Bake at 325° for 3 hours or until brisket is tender. Cut brisket across grain into thin slices. Cut potatoes in half. Arrange brisket and vegetables on a serving platter; set aside, and keep warm. Pour 1½ cups cooking liquid into a saucepan.

Combine remaining 1 tablespoon flour and 2 tablespoons water; stir well. Add to cooking liquid. Bring to a boil; cook, stirring constantly, 2 minutes or until thickened. Serve gravy with brisket and vegetables. Yield: 6 servings.

PER SERVING: 278 CALORIES (21% FROM FAT)
FAT 6.5G (SATURATED FAT 2.1G)
PROTEIN 30.2G   CARBOHYDRATE 24.4G
CHOLESTEROL 75MG   SODIUM 337MG

FRUITED CIDER ROAST

1 (3½-pound) lean boneless top round roast
¼ teaspoon salt
¼ teaspoon pepper
Vegetable cooking spray
6 cups unsweetened apple cider
3 cups cider vinegar
1 (6-ounce) package dried apricot halves,
    chopped
½ cup raisins
¼ cup firmly packed dark brown sugar
¼ teaspoon ground allspice

Trim fat from roast. Sprinkle roast with salt and pepper. Coat a Dutch oven with cooking spray; place over medium-high heat until hot. Add roast, and cook until browned on all sides.

Combine cider and vinegar; pour over roast. Bring to a boil; cover, reduce heat, and simmer 3 to 3½ hours or until roast is tender. Transfer roast to a serving platter; set aside, and keep warm.

Skim fat from pan juices. Reserve 2 cups juices; discard remaining juices. Return 2 cups juices to Dutch oven; add apricot and remaining 3 ingredients. Cook over medium-high heat 8 to 10 minutes or until thickened, stirring often. Serve fruit mixture with roast. Yield: 12 servings.

PER SERVING: 253 CALORIES (20% FROM FAT)
FAT 5.6G (SATURATED FAT 1.9G)
PROTEIN 28.4G CARBOHYDRATE 22.5G
CHOLESTEROL 73MG SODIUM 107MG

Roasting Tips

• Use an oven thermometer to determine your oven's accuracy. Then adjust the temperature according to your owner's manual.
• Use a meat thermometer to measure the internal temperature of the roast as it cooks.
• Use a roasting pan with a rack so that the fat drips down and air circulates around the roast. For easier cleanup, line the pan with aluminum foil.

ROAST VEAL WITH MUSHROOM SAUCE

Crimini mushrooms are the brown cousins to white button mushrooms. Substitute white button mushrooms if crimini are not available.

1 (2-pound) boneless veal round roast
½ teaspoon salt-free lemon-pepper seasoning
Vegetable cooking spray
1 teaspoon olive oil
½ cup diced shallot
4 ounces fresh shiitake mushroom caps, sliced
4 ounces sliced fresh mushrooms
1 (8-ounce) package fresh crimini mushrooms,
    sliced
1 cup canned no-salt-added beef broth
½ cup dry sherry
¼ cup minced fresh parsley
¾ teaspoon dried tarragon
¼ teaspoon salt
Fresh parsley sprigs (optional)

Trim fat from roast. Sprinkle lemon-pepper seasoning over entire surface of roast. Place roast on a rack in a roasting pan coated with cooking spray. Insert meat thermometer into thickest part of roast, if desired. Bake at 450° for 40 minutes or until meat thermometer registers 160°.

Let roast stand 10 minutes; cut into thin slices. Arrange slices on a serving platter, and keep warm.

Coat a large nonstick skillet with cooking spray; add olive oil. Place over medium-high heat until hot. Add shallot and next 3 ingredients; sauté until tender.

Add broth and next 4 ingredients to mushroom mixture. Bring mixture to a boil; reduce heat, and simmer, uncovered, 20 minutes, stirring often. Spoon mushroom mixture over veal. Garnish with fresh parsley sprigs, if desired. Yield: 8 servings.

PER SERVING: 202 CALORIES (29% FROM FAT)
FAT 6.5G (SATURATED FAT 1.7G)
PROTEIN 28.6G CARBOHYDRATE 6.1G
CHOLESTEROL 100MG SODIUM 155MG

Roast Pork with Apricot-Prune Stuffing

ROAST PORK WITH APRICOT-PRUNE STUFFING

¾ cup Madeira wine
½ cup chopped pitted prunes
½ cup chopped dried apricot
¾ teaspoon salt, divided
½ teaspoon dried rosemary, crushed
1 (3-pound) lean, boneless pork loin
¼ teaspoon pepper
Vegetable cooking spray
Fresh rosemary sprigs (optional)

Combine first 3 ingredients in a bowl; stir well. Cover and let stand 30 minutes. Drain, reserving Madeira. Combine prunes, apricot, ¼ teaspoon salt, and ½ teaspoon rosemary; stir well. Set aside.

Trim fat from pork. To butterfly pork, slice loin lengthwise, cutting to, but not through, other side. Open halves, laying pork flat. Slice each half lengthwise, cutting to, but not through, other side; open flat. Place heavy-duty plastic wrap over pork, and flatten to an even thickness, using a meat mallet or rolling pin. Spread prune mixture down center of pork to within ½ inch of sides.

Roll up pork, jellyroll fashion, starting with short side. Secure with heavy string. Sprinkle remaining ½ teaspoon salt and pepper over pork.

Place pork, seam side down, on rack of a broiler pan coated with cooking spray; insert meat thermometer into thickest portion of pork. Bake at 350° for 1½ hours or until thermometer registers 160°; baste with reserved Madeira. Place roast on a serving platter; let stand 15 minutes before slicing. Garnish with fresh rosemary, if desired. Yield: 12 servings.

PER SERVING: 176 CALORIES (21% FROM FAT)
FAT 4.2G (SATURATED FAT 1.4G)
PROTEIN 24.9G   CARBOHYDRATE 8.8G
CHOLESTEROL 79MG   SODIUM 210MG

Fresh Ham with Maple Syrup-Bourbon Glaze

FRESH HAM WITH MAPLE SYRUP-BOURBON GLAZE

½ cup maple syrup
2 tablespoons brown sugar
3 tablespoons bourbon
½ teaspoon ground ginger
½ teaspoon ground allspice
1 (6¾-pound) fresh ham, boned
1 clove garlic, minced
2 teaspoons salt, divided
1 teaspoon pepper, divided
Vegetable cooking spray
8 medium-size sweet potatoes, cooked
½ cup firmly packed brown sugar
2 tablespoons plus 2 teaspoons reduced-calorie
   stick margarine
Fresh thyme sprigs (optional)
Fresh cranberries (optional)

Combine first 3 ingredients in a small saucepan; bring to boil. Reduce heat to low, and simmer 5 minutes or until slightly thickened. Remove from heat; stir in ginger and allspice. Cool slightly.

Trim fat from outside and inside surfaces of ham. Spread ⅓ cup syrup mixture and garlic over inside surface of ham; sprinkle with 1 teaspoon salt and ½ teaspoon pepper. Reshape ham to original shape. Secure at 2-inch intervals with heavy string.

Spread 3 tablespoons syrup mixture over ham; sprinkle with remaining 1 teaspoon salt and remaining ½ teaspoon pepper.

Place ham on a rack of a broiler pan coated with cooking spray; insert meat thermometer into thickest portion of ham. Bake at 350° for 2 hours or until thermometer registers 160°, basting with remaining syrup mixture after 1 hour.

Place ham on a serving platter; cover with aluminum foil, and let stand 15 minutes before slicing.

Cut warm potatoes in half; scoop out pulp, and place in a mixing bowl. Discard skins. Add brown sugar and margarine to potato; beat at medium speed of an electric mixer until smooth.

Pipe sweet potato mixture around ham. If desired, garnish with fresh thyme and cranberries. Slice ham, and serve. Yield: 15 servings.

Note: Cook sweet potatoes in boiling water 45 minutes to 1 hour or until tender. Or bake potatoes at 400° for 45 minutes or until tender.

PER SERVING: 405 CALORIES (30% FROM FAT)
FAT 13.5G (SATURATED FAT 4.3G)
PROTEIN 34.0G CARBOHYDRATE 35.3G
CHOLESTEROL 107MG SODIUM 420MG

FYI

The ham recipe on this page calls for a fresh ham. Because fresh ham is an uncured leg of pork, it will be grayish instead of pink. Use a meat thermometer to check for doneness of the ham.

The bone of a fresh ham is tricky to remove, so ask your butcher to do it for you.

CROWN ROAST OF LAMB WITH WILD RICE-RISOTTO STUFFING

3½ cups water
1¼ cups wild rice, uncooked
2 teaspoons salt, divided
1 tablespoon plus 1 teaspoon olive oil, divided
2 cups thinly sliced shiitake mushroom caps
2 teaspoons herbes de Provence
1½ teaspoons pepper, divided
1 (16-rib) crown roast of lamb
Olive oil-flavored vegetable cooking spray
5 cups low-sodium chicken broth
1½ cups chopped onion
1 cup diced celery
1 cup Arborio or other short-grain rice, uncooked
1 cup frozen English peas, thawed
2 teaspoons chopped fresh thyme
Fresh tarragon sprigs (optional)

Bring water to a boil in a saucepan. Add wild rice and ½ teaspoon salt; cover, reduce heat, and simmer 50 minutes or until tender. Drain; set aside.

Heat 2 teaspoons oil in a small nonstick skillet over high heat. Add mushrooms; sauté 5 minutes or until browned. Remove from heat; stir in ¼ teaspoon salt.

Combine 1 teaspoon salt, herbes de Provence, and ¾ teaspoon pepper. Lightly coat roast with cooking spray; rub herb mixture over roast. Place roast, bone side up, on a rack of a broiler pan coated with cooking spray; insert meat thermometer into thickest portion of roast, making sure it does not touch bone. Cover bones with aluminum foil, and place a ball of foil in center of roast. Place in a 500° oven; immediately reduce oven temperature to 400°; bake 45 minutes or until thermometer registers 135° (medium-rare). Place roast on a large serving platter; cover with aluminum foil, and set aside.

Place broth in a medium saucepan; bring to a simmer (do not boil). Keep warm over low heat.

Heat remaining 2 teaspoons oil in a large saucepan over medium heat. Add onion and celery; sauté

1 minute. Add Arborio rice; cook, stirring constantly, 1 minute. Add wild rice and ½ cup warm broth; cook, stirring constantly, 1 minute or until liquid is nearly absorbed. Add remaining warm broth, ½ cup at a time, stirring constantly until each portion of broth is nearly absorbed before adding next (about 20 minutes total). Stir in remaining ¼ teaspoon salt, remaining ¾ teaspoon pepper, mushrooms, peas, and thyme. Cook until thoroughly heated.

Uncover roast; remove foil ball. Spoon risotto into center of roast (if all of risotto does not fit, serve remaining risotto in a bowl). Garnish with fresh tarragon, if desired. Serve 1 cup risotto with each 2-rib chop serving. Yield: 8 servings.

PER SERVING: 456 CALORIES (30% FROM FAT)
FAT 15.0G (SATURATED FAT 4.6G)
PROTEIN 32.4G   CARBOHYDRATE 47.6G
CHOLESTEROL 77MG   SODIUM 741MG

Crown Roast of Lamb with Wild Rice-Risotto Stuffing

Italian Chicken Rolls

ITALIAN CHICKEN ROLLS

6 (4-ounce) skinned, boned chicken breast
    halves
¼ teaspoon salt
¼ teaspoon pepper
½ cup chopped bottled roasted sweet red
    pepper
⅓ cup tub-style light process cream cheese,
    softened
¼ cup pesto
¾ cup crushed corn flakes cereal
3 tablespoons chopped fresh parsley
½ teaspoon paprika
Vegetable cooking spray
Fresh thyme sprigs (optional)

Place chicken between two sheets of heavy-duty
plastic wrap; flatten to ¼-inch thickness, using a
meat mallet or rolling pin. Sprinkle with salt and ¼
teaspoon pepper; set aside.

Combine red pepper, cream cheese, and pesto,
stirring until smooth; spread mixture evenly over
chicken breasts. Roll up, jellyroll fashion; secure
with wooden picks.

Combine crushed cereal, parsley, and paprika.
Dredge chicken in cereal mixture. Place in an 11-
x 7- x 1½-inch baking dish coated with cooking
spray. Bake, uncovered, at 350° for 35 minutes; let
stand 10 minutes. Remove wooden picks from
chicken, and slice each roll into 6 rounds. Garnish
with thyme sprigs, if desired. Yield: 6 servings.

Note: It's easy to crush the cereal in a plastic
zip-top bag with a rolling pin. You'll need about
3 cups cereal to get ¾ cup crumbs. Or look for a
package of cornflake crumbs in the baking section
of your supermarket.

PER SERVING: 253 CALORIES (32% FROM FAT)
FAT 9.0G (SATURATED FAT 2.6G)
PROTEIN 29.7G CARBOHYDRATE 12.1G
CHOLESTEROL 75MG SODIUM 506MG

GRECIAN CORNISH HENS

2 (1-pound) Cornish hens, skinned
¼ cup commercial fat-free Italian dressing
¼ cup lemon juice, divided
1¼ cups water
¼ teaspoon salt
⅔ cup basmati rice, uncooked
3 tablespoons pine nuts, toasted
2 tablespoons chopped fresh parsley
2 teaspoons dried basil
1 teaspoon dried thyme
½ teaspoon pepper
Vegetable cooking spray
12 grape leaves
Lemon slices (optional)

Remove giblets from hens; reserve for another
use. Rinse hens under cold water, and pat dry. Split
each hen in half lengthwise, using an electric knife.

Place hens in a large heavy-duty, zip-top plastic
bag. Combine Italian dressing and 2 tablespoons
lemon juice. Pour over hens; seal bag, and shake
until hens are well coated. Marinate in refrigerator
8 hours, turning bag occasionally.

Bring water and salt to a boil in a saucepan; stir
in rice. Cover, reduce heat, and simmer 20 minutes
or until liquid is absorbed and rice is tender.

Combine cooked rice, 1 tablespoon lemon juice,
pine nuts, and next 4 ingredients; stir well. Spoon
into an 11- x 7- x 1½-inch baking dish coated with
cooking spray.

Remove hens from marinade; place hens on rice
mixture, and drizzle marinade over hens. Cover
hens with grape leaves; drizzle remaining 1 tablespoon lemon juice over grape leaves. Cover and
bake at 350° for 1 hour or until hens are done.

To serve, remove and discard top layer of grape
leaves that may have darkened. Place remaining
grape leaves on individual serving plates, and top
with rice mixture and hens. Garnish with lemon
slices, if desired. Yield: 4 servings.

PER SERVING: 310 CALORIES (23% FROM FAT)
FAT 7.8G (SATURATED FAT 1.5G)
PROTEIN 27.9G CARBOHYDRATE 32.0G
CHOLESTEROL 76MG SODIUM 485MG

Curried Turkey Ballottine

CURRIED TURKEY BALLOTTINE

1 (5-pound) whole turkey breast, skinned and
   boned
2¾ cups plus 3 tablespoons water, divided
¼ cup raisins
¼ cup dried apricots
1 tablespoon olive oil, divided
1 cup diced onion
½ cup diced sweet red pepper
½ cup diced green pepper
½ cup diced celery
3 cloves garlic, crushed
½ cup couscous, uncooked
2 teaspoons caraway seeds
1½ teaspoons ground cumin

1½ teaspoons ground coriander
½ teaspoon salt
¼ teaspoon pepper
⅛ teaspoon hot sauce
1 cup sliced carrot
1 cup dry vermouth
1 cup canned low-sodium chicken broth
½ cup sliced onion
½ cup sliced celery
Watercress
1 teaspoon curry powder
2 teaspoons cornstarch
¼ teaspoon salt
⅛ teaspoon pepper

Trim fat from turkey breast; remove tendons. Place outer side of turkey breast on heavy-duty plastic wrap. Starting from center, slice horizontally through thickest portion of each side of breast almost to, but not through, outer edges. Flip cut pieces over to enlarge breast. Place heavy-duty plastic wrap over turkey; pound turkey to a more even thickness, using a meat mallet or rolling pin.

Combine 2 cups water, raisins, and apricots in a small saucepan; bring mixture to a boil. Cover, reduce heat, and simmer 5 minutes or until apricots are tender. Drain and set aside.

Heat 2 teaspoons olive oil in a saucepan over medium heat. Add diced onion, and cook 10 minutes, stirring occasionally. Add diced red pepper and next 3 ingredients; sauté 1 minute. Add raisin mixture to onion mixture, and set aside.

Bring ¾ cup water to a boil in a small saucepan. Remove from heat. Add couscous; cover and let stand 5 minutes or until liquid is absorbed and couscous is tender. Fluff with a fork.

Combine onion mixture, couscous, caraway seeds, and next 5 ingredients; toss well. Spread mixture over turkey breast to within 2 inches of edges; roll up turkey breast, jellyroll fashion, starting with short side. Tie securely at 2-inch intervals with heavy string.

Heat remaining 1 teaspoon oil in a large roasting pan over medium-high heat. Add turkey; brown on all sides. Add carrot and next 4 ingredients. Insert meat thermometer into thickest portion of turkey roll. Cover and bake at 350° for 1½ hours or until meat thermometer registers 170°.

Transfer turkey roll to a large serving platter lined with watercress, reserving pan drippings and vegetables. Let turkey roll stand 10 minutes. Remove string; cut turkey roll into 13 slices.

Strain pan drippings and vegetables; discard vegetables. Pour liquid into a saucepan; bring to a boil over medium-high heat. Cook 8 minutes or until liquid is reduced to 1½ cups; set aside.

Place curry powder in a small saucepan over medium-high heat. Cook, stirring constantly, 45 seconds. Add reserved 1½ cups cooking liquid to saucepan.

Combine cornstarch and remaining 3 tablespoons water; stir well. Add to cooking liquid in saucepan; stir well. Bring to a boil; cook, stirring constantly,

1 minute. Stir in ¼ teaspoon salt and ⅛ teaspoon pepper. Serve 2 tablespoons sauce with each slice of turkey roll. Yield: 13 servings.

PER SERVING: 238 CALORIES (20% FROM FAT)
FAT 5.3G (SATURATED FAT 1.4G)
PROTEIN 36.9G   CARBOHYDRATE 8.7G
CHOLESTEROL 83MG   SODIUM 236MG

Roll up the turkey breast, jellyroll fashion, starting with short side of turkey.

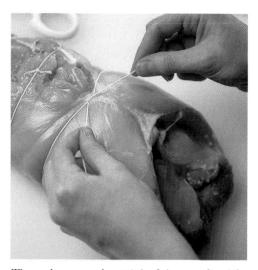

Tie turkey securely at 2-inch intervals with heavy string.

HOLIDAY TURKEY CUTLETS

1 pound turkey breast cutlets, cut into 8 pieces
3 tablespoons all-purpose flour
2 teaspoons vegetable oil
¾ cup chopped onion
¾ cup fresh cranberries
½ cup canned low-sodium chicken broth
2 tablespoons sugar
2 tablespoons red wine vinegar
2 tablespoons commercial fat-free Catalina
    dressing
¼ teaspoon salt
Fresh sage sprigs (optional)
Orange slices (optional)

Place turkey between two sheets of heavy-duty plastic wrap; flatten to ⅛-inch thickness, using a meat mallet or rolling pin. Dredge turkey in flour.

Heat oil in a large nonstick skillet over medium heat until hot. Add cutlets, and cook 2 minutes on each side or until browned. Transfer to a serving platter; keep warm. Wipe drippings from skillet with a paper towel.

Place skillet over medium-high heat until hot. Add onion, and sauté until tender. Add cranberries and next 5 ingredients; bring to a boil. Reduce heat, and simmer 3 to 4 minutes or until cranberries pop.

Spoon cranberry mixture over cutlets, and serve immediately. If desired, garnish with fresh sage sprigs and orange slices. Yield: 4 servings.

PER SERVING: 218 CALORIES (17% FROM FAT)
FAT 4.1G (SATURATED FAT 1.0G)
PROTEIN 27.5G   CARBOHYDRATE 15.7G
CHOLESTEROL 68MG   SODIUM 295MG

Holiday Turkey Cutlets

Crawfish Fettuccine

CRAWFISH FETTUCCINE

¼ cup reduced-calorie stick margarine
1¾ cups chopped onion
1½ cups chopped sweet red pepper
1½ cups chopped green pepper
1 cup chopped green onions
4 cloves garlic, minced
¼ cup all-purpose flour
1½ cups fat-free milk
½ pound light process cheese spread, cubed
1½ pounds cooked, peeled crawfish or shrimp
1 tablespoon low-sodium Worcestershire sauce
¼ teaspoon black pepper
¼ teaspoon ground red pepper
9 cups hot cooked fettuccine (about 16 ounces uncooked), cooked without salt or fat
Fresh parsley sprigs (optional)
Fresh crawfish or shrimp (optional)

Melt margarine in a Dutch oven over medium-high heat. Add onion and next 4 ingredients; sauté 5 minutes. Stir in flour; gradually add milk, stirring with a wire whisk. Add cheese, stirring until cheese melts. Stir in 1½ pounds crawfish and next 3 ingredients; cook until heated. Add pasta, and toss well. If desired, garnish with parsley and crawfish. Yield: 9 (1½-cup) servings.

Note: You can make Crawfish Fettuccine ahead. To reheat, cover and bake at 350° for 30 minutes.

PER SERVING: 412 CALORIES (18% FROM FAT)
FAT 8.3G (SATURATED FAT 2.6G)
PROTEIN 31.6G   CARBOHYDRATE 51.1G
CHOLESTEROL 149MG   SODIUM 547MG

Spicy Shrimp Creole

SPICY SHRIMP CREOLE

1 pound unpeeled medium-size fresh
   shrimp
Olive oil-flavored vegetable cooking
   spray
1 cup chopped onion
1 cup chopped green pepper
½ teaspoon dried crushed red pepper
6 cloves garlic, minced
2 (14½-ounce) cans Cajun-style stewed
   tomatoes, undrained
5 cups hot cooked rice (cooked without salt
   or fat)

Peel and devein shrimp; set aside.

Coat a large nonstick skillet with cooking spray; place over medium-high heat until hot. Add onion and next 3 ingredients; sauté until tender. Add tomatoes. Bring to a boil; reduce heat, and simmer, uncovered, 10 minutes, stirring occasionally. Add shrimp. Cover and cook 5 minutes or until shrimp turn pink. Serve over rice. Yield: 5 servings.

PER SERVING: 362 CALORIES (4% FROM FAT)
FAT 1.7G (SATURATED FAT 0.3G)
PROTEIN 20.0G   CARBOHYDRATE 66.4G
CHOLESTEROL 103MG   SODIUM 748MG

CREAMY LOBSTER WITH ANGEL HAIR PASTA

(pictured on page 68)

2 quarts water
2 (8-ounce) fresh or frozen lobster tails, thawed
8 ounces angel hair pasta, uncooked
¾ cup sliced fresh mushrooms
⅓ cup chopped green onions
⅓ cup dry white wine
1 large clove garlic, minced
2 tablespoons reduced-calorie stick margarine
2 tablespoons all-purpose flour
1 cup fat-free milk
⅓ cup nonfat sour cream
2 tablespoons grated Parmesan cheese
½ teaspoon paprika
Fresh parsley sprigs (optional)

Bring water to a boil in a large saucepan; add lobster tails. Cover, reduce heat, and simmer 6 minutes. Drain; rinse with cold water. Split and clean tails; cut meat into bite-size pieces.

Cook pasta according to package directions, omitting salt and fat. Drain well. Set pasta aside, and keep warm.

Combine mushrooms and next 3 ingredients in a large nonstick skillet. Bring to a boil. Reduce heat, and simmer, uncovered, until liquid evaporates.

Add margarine, stirring to melt. Add flour, and cook, stirring constantly, 1 minute. Gradually stir in milk. Cook over medium heat, stirring constantly, until mixture thickens and begins to boil. Stir in lobster and sour cream; cook 1 additional minute or until thoroughly heated. Spoon over pasta; sprinkle with cheese and paprika. Garnish with parsley sprigs, if desired. Yield: 4 servings.

PER SERVING: 390 CALORIES (15% FROM FAT)
FAT 6.3G (SATURATED FAT 1.5G)
PROTEIN 28.8G CARBOHYDRATE 52.8G
CHOLESTEROL 59MG SODIUM 464MG

SPICY CRUSTED SWORDFISH WITH CITRUS-WALNUT SAUCE

2 tablespoons Italian-seasoned breadcrumbs
½ teaspoon ground cinnamon
½ teaspoon ground ginger
½ teaspoon pepper
¼ teaspoon salt
¼ teaspoon ground cumin
1 tablespoon extra-virgin olive oil, divided
4 (6-ounce) swordfish steaks
1 cup water
⅔ cup couscous, uncooked
½ teaspoon grated lemon rind
1 tablespoon fresh lemon juice
¼ teaspoon salt
1 tablespoon chopped fresh mint
½ cup currants or raisins
1 teaspoon grated orange rind
½ cup fresh orange juice
2 tablespoons coarsely chopped toasted walnuts
1 tablespoon honey
Cherry tomatoes (optional)

Combine first 6 ingredients. Stir in 1 teaspoon oil. Rub spice mixture over both sides of swordfish. Cover and chill 30 minutes.

Bring water to a boil in a saucepan; gradually stir in couscous. Remove from heat; cover and let stand 5 minutes. Fluff with a fork. Stir in lemon rind and next 3 ingredients. Set aside; keep warm.

Combine 1 teaspoon oil, currants, and next 4 ingredients in a small saucepan. Bring to a simmer. Remove from heat; keep warm.

Heat remaining 1 teaspoon oil in a large nonstick skillet over medium-high heat. Add swordfish, and cook 5 minutes on each side or until fish flakes easily when tested with a fork. Serve each steak with ½ cup couscous, and drizzle with ¼ cup sauce. Garnish with cherry tomatoes, if desired. Yield: 4 servings.

PER SERVING: 399 CALORIES (28% FROM FAT)
FAT 12.5G (SATURATED FAT 2.5G)
PROTEIN 36.5G CARBOHYDRATE 36.0G
CHOLESTEROL 64MG SODIUM 544MG

Marsala Potatoes au Gratin (recipe on page 92)

SIDE-DISH FAVORITES

Each part of a holiday meal deserves some extra attention, and side dishes are no exception. Vivid memories of holidays past often include remembrances of sweet potato casserole, bread stuffing, or potato latkes. Mothers and grandmothers have prepared such favorites for years, and now you can prepare the same tasty dishes minus the extra fat and calories.

You can embellish simple vegetables for seasonal meals with little effort. Grapefruit Salad with Champagne Dressing (page 88), Sesame Broccoli (page 89), and Apricot-Ginger Carrots (page 90) are perfect examples of basic dishes that have been given a flavor boost. They'll add texture, taste, and festive color to your holiday table.

LAYERED CRANBERRY-APPLESAUCE SALAD

2 envelopes unflavored gelatin
1¾ cups water
½ cup sugar
1 (12-ounce) can frozen cranberry juice
 concentrate, thawed and undiluted
1¼ cups sliced fresh strawberries
1¼ cups unsweetened applesauce
1 cup low-fat sour cream
¼ cup chopped walnuts
2 tablespoons powdered sugar

Sprinkle gelatin over water in a saucepan; let stand 1 minute. Stir in ½ cup sugar. Cook over medium heat, stirring until gelatin and sugar dissolve. Remove from heat.

Set aside 2 teaspoons juice concentrate; add remaining concentrate to gelatin mixture. Stir in strawberries and applesauce. Pour half of mixture into an 11- x 7- x 1½-inch baking dish. Cover and chill until firm. Reserve remaining gelatin mixture; do not chill.

Combine reserved 2 teaspoons juice concentrate, sour cream, walnuts, and powdered sugar; stir well. Spread over firm gelatin layer. Gradually pour reserved gelatin mixture over sour cream mixture. Cover and chill until firm. To serve, cut salad lengthwise into 3 equal pieces; cut each piece crosswise into 5 equal pieces. Yield: 15 servings.

PER SERVING: 120 CALORIES (24% FROM FAT)
FAT 3.2G (SATURATED FAT 1.3G)
PROTEIN 2.2G CARBOHYDRATE 21.8G
CHOLESTEROL 6MG SODIUM 9MG

HEARTS OF PALM SALAD WITH FRUIT

This salad is bursting with color, texture, and unexpected flavors.

¼ cup evaporated skimmed milk
3 tablespoons nonfat mayonnaise
2½ tablespoons unsweetened orange juice
2 tablespoons reduced-fat creamy peanut
 butter spread
¾ teaspoon sugar
½ teaspoon ground ginger
2 heads Bibb lettuce, divided
1 cup sliced fresh strawberries
¾ cup sliced celery
1 (14.4-ounce) can hearts of palm, drained and
 sliced
1 (11-ounce) can mandarin orange segments in
 light syrup, drained
1 head radicchio
2 tablespoons coarsely chopped unsalted
 peanuts

Combine first 6 ingredients in container of an electric blender or food processor; cover and process until smooth. Transfer mayonnaise mixture to a small bowl; cover and chill at least 30 minutes.

Tear 1 head Bibb lettuce into bite-size pieces. Combine torn lettuce, strawberries, and next 3 ingredients; toss gently.

Separate remaining head Bibb lettuce and radicchio into leaves. Arrange leaves on six individual salad plates.

Spoon strawberry mixture evenly over lettuce leaves. Drizzle 2 tablespoons mayonnaise mixture over each salad. Sprinkle evenly with peanuts, and serve immediately. Yield: 6 (1-cup) servings.

PER SERVING: 161 CALORIES (26% FROM FAT)
FAT 4.7G (SATURATED FAT 0.7G)
PROTEIN 5.8G CARBOHYDRATE 27.2G
CHOLESTEROL 0MG SODIUM 259MG

Hearts of Palm Salad with Fruit

Grapefruit Salad with Champagne Dressing

You can substitute any other dry champagne (one that isn't sweet) for the brut in this recipe.

¼ cup plus 2 tablespoons brut champagne
2 tablespoons raspberry vinegar
2 tablespoons honey
1 tablespoon vegetable oil
2 teaspoons Dijon mustard
4 cups tightly packed torn romaine lettuce
3 cups fresh grapefruit sections (about 3
    medium grapefruit)
2 cups halved fresh strawberries
½ cup vertically sliced purple onion

Combine first 5 ingredients in a small bowl; stir with a wire whisk until blended. Cover and chill.

Combine lettuce and remaining 3 ingredients in a large bowl, and toss gently. Pour dressing over lettuce mixture; toss gently. Serve immediately. Yield: 6 (1½-cup) servings.

PER SERVING: 109 CALORIES (22% FROM FAT)
FAT 2.7G (SATURATED FAT 0.4G)
PROTEIN 1.6G CARBOHYDRATE 19.0G
CHOLESTEROL 0MG SODIUM 54MG

To section a grapefruit, gently slide the knife between the membrane and the grapefruit section on both sides; lift out the citrus section.

Wild Rice and Pecan Salad

2½ cups water
⅛ teaspoon salt
½ cup wild rice, uncooked
½ cup long-grain brown rice, uncooked
¾ cup diced carrot
½ cup frozen English peas, thawed
½ cup diced celery
½ cup diced sweet red pepper
⅓ cup diced purple onion
⅓ cup finely chopped green onions
⅓ cup finely chopped fresh parsley
¼ cup lemon juice
1 tablespoon olive oil
¼ teaspoon salt
⅛ teaspoon pepper
1 clove garlic, minced
2 tablespoons chopped pecans

Bring water and salt to a boil in a saucepan. Gradually stir in rices. Cover, reduce heat, and simmer 40 minutes or until rice is tender. Drain and set aside.

Arrange carrot in a steamer basket; place over boiling water. Cover and steam 3 minutes. Add English peas; cook 1 minute, and drain.

Combine rice mixture, carrot mixture, celery, and next 4 ingredients in a bowl. Combine lemon juice and next 4 ingredients in a jar. Cover tightly, and shake vigorously. Pour over rice mixture; toss well. Top with pecans. Serve chilled or at room temperature. Yield: 12 (½-cup) servings.

PER SERVING: 86 CALORIES (23% FROM FAT)
FAT 2.2G (SATURATED FAT 0.3G)
PROTEIN 2.3G CARBOHYDRATE 15.0G
CHOLESTEROL 0MG SODIUM 89MG

Sesame Broccoli

SESAME BROCCOLI

Team this easy side dish with steak and potatoes for a quick, casual holiday supper.

1½ pounds fresh broccoli
1 teaspoon vegetable oil
1 tablespoon sesame seeds
1 tablespoon sugar
1 tablespoon lemon juice
1 tablespoon low-sodium soy sauce

Remove broccoli leaves, and cut off tough ends; discard. Cut broccoli into spears, and arrange in a steamer basket over boiling water. Cover; steam 7 minutes or until crisp-tender. Drain; place in a bowl.

Heat oil in a small saucepan over medium heat. Add sesame seeds, and sauté until seeds are lightly browned. Add sugar, lemon juice, and soy sauce; bring to a boil. Drizzle over broccoli, tossing gently to coat. Yield: 4 (1-cup) servings.

PER SERVING: 67 CALORIES (35% FROM FAT)
FAT 2.6G (SATURATED FAT 0.4G)
PROTEIN 3.7G   CARBOHYDRATE 9.7G
CHOLESTEROL 0MG   SODIUM 149MG

APRICOT-GINGER CARROTS

Crystallized ginger is gingerroot that has been cooked in a sugar syrup and coated with coarse sugar. It adds a sweeter ginger flavor than gingerroot and can be used in savory dishes as well as in desserts.

1 (2-pound) package fresh baby carrots
1 cup water
1 (10-ounce) jar low-sugar apricot preserves
2 tablespoons stick margarine
2 teaspoons minced crystallized ginger

Combine carrots and water in a saucepan; bring to a boil. Cover, reduce heat, and simmer 12 minutes or until carrots are tender. Drain carrots, and transfer to a bowl.

Combine preserves, margarine, and ginger in saucepan. Cook over low heat, stirring constantly, 2 minutes or until preserves melt. Return carrots to saucepan; toss lightly. Cook until thoroughly heated. Yield: 10 (½-cup) servings.

PER SERVING: 126 CALORIES (17% FROM FAT)
FAT 2.4G (SATURATED FAT 0.5G)
PROTEIN 0.9G   CARBOHYDRATE 25.8G
CHOLESTEROL 0MG   SODIUM 59MG

SESAME SUGAR SNAP PEAS

Vegetable cooking spray
1 teaspoon dark sesame oil
2 (8-ounce) packages frozen Sugar Snap peas
1 (8-ounce) can sliced water chestnuts, drained
¼ cup low-sodium soy sauce
3 tablespoons brown sugar
1 tablespoon peeled, chopped gingerroot
2 teaspoons cornstarch

Coat a large nonstick skillet with cooking spray; add oil. Place over medium-high heat until hot.

Add peas and water chestnuts; sauté 4 to 5 minutes or until peas are crisp-tender.

Combine soy sauce and remaining 3 ingredients, stirring until smooth. Add to vegetable mixture. Bring to a boil; cook, stirring constantly, 2 minutes or until thickened and bubbly. Yield: 6 (¾-cup) servings.

PER SERVING: 90 CALORIES (11% FROM FAT)
FAT 1.1G (SATURATED FAT 0.1G)
PROTEIN 2.4G   CARBOHYDRATE 16.7G
CHOLESTEROL 0MG   SODIUM 268MG

POTATO LATKES

Latkes, or potato pancakes, are served traditionally during Hanukkah.

3 cups peeled, cubed baking potato (about 1¼ pounds)
2 tablespoons all-purpose flour
½ teaspoon salt
¼ teaspoon baking powder
⅛ teaspoon pepper
2 egg whites
1 small onion, quartered
1 tablespoon vegetable oil, divided
¼ cup plus 2 tablespoons nonfat sour cream

Position knife blade in food processor bowl; add first 7 ingredients. Pulse 20 times or until potato is very finely chopped.

Heat ½ teaspoon vegetable oil in a large nonstick skillet over medium-high heat. For each pancake, spoon about 1 heaping tablespoon batter into skillet. Cook 1½ minutes on each side or until browned. Repeat procedure until all oil and batter have been used. For each serving, top 4 pancakes with 1 tablespoon sour cream. Yield: 6 servings.

PER SERVING: 113 CALORIES (19% FROM FAT)
FAT 2.4G (SATURATED FAT 0.4G)
PROTEIN 4.2G   CARBOHYDRATE 18.7G
CHOLESTEROL 0MG   SODIUM 245MG

Potato Latkes

MARSALA POTATOES AU GRATIN

(pictured on page 84)

2 large onions
Vegetable cooking spray
2 teaspoons vegetable oil
1⅓ cups sweet Marsala wine
1 teaspoon dried thyme
2½ pounds medium-size round red potatoes,
    peeled and cut into ⅛-inch slices
2 tablespoons all-purpose flour
¾ teaspoon salt
½ cup fat-free milk
2 tablespoons grated Parmesan cheese

Cut each onion in half lengthwise, and cut each half crosswise into ⅛-inch-thick slices. Coat a large saucepan with cooking spray; add oil, and place over medium heat until hot. Add onion slices, and sauté 10 minutes. Add wine, and cook 20 minutes or until liquid is nearly absorbed, stirring often. Remove from heat, and stir in thyme. Set aside.

Cook potato slices in boiling water 8 minutes or until crisp-tender; drain. Pour cold water over potato slices, and drain well.

Arrange one-third of potato slices in a 13- x 9- x 2-inch baking dish coated with cooking spray; spoon half of onion mixture over potato slices. Repeat procedure with remaining potato slices and onion mixture, ending with potato slices.

Place flour and salt in a bowl. Gradually add milk, stirring with a wire whisk until smooth. Pour milk mixture evenly over potato slices, and sprinkle with Parmesan cheese. Cover with aluminum foil; cut three 1-inch slits in foil. Bake at 350° for 45 minutes. Uncover and bake 15 additional minutes. Yield: 7 (1-cup) servings.

PER SERVING: 156 CALORIES (13% FROM FAT)
FAT 2.2G (SATURATED FAT 0.6G)
PROTEIN 4.6G   CARBOHYDRATE 30.1G
CHOLESTEROL 1MG   SODIUM 300MG

ORANGE SWEET POTATO SOUFFLÉ

2 cups peeled, cubed sweet potato
¾ cup evaporated skimmed milk
½ cup fat-free egg substitute
¼ cup firmly packed brown sugar
1 tablespoon frozen orange juice concentrate,
    thawed and undiluted
1 tablespoon Triple Sec or other
    orange-flavored liqueur
½ teaspoon ground cinnamon
½ teaspoon ground allspice
¼ teaspoon salt
¼ teaspoon ground nutmeg
3 egg whites

Cook sweet potato in boiling water to cover 15 minutes or until tender; drain. Transfer sweet potato to a large bowl. Beat at medium speed of an electric mixer until smooth. Add milk and next 8 ingredients; beat at low speed until blended.

Beat egg whites at high speed of mixer until stiff peaks form. Fold one-third of beaten egg whites into sweet potato mixture; fold in remaining egg whites. Spoon mixture into an ungreased 2-quart soufflé dish. Bake, uncovered, at 325° for 55 minutes or until golden. Serve immediately. Yield: 6 servings.

PER SERVING: 132 CALORIES (2% FROM FAT)
FAT 0.3G (SATURATED FAT 0.1G)
PROTEIN 6.9G   CARBOHYDRATE 25.8G
CHOLESTEROL 1MG   SODIUM 200MG

FRUITED ACORN SQUASH

2 medium acorn squash (about 2 pounds)
Vegetable cooking spray
¾ cup canned crushed pineapple in juice, drained
¾ cup peeled, chopped orange
3 tablespoons brown sugar
½ teaspoon ground cinnamon
Orange rind curls (optional)
Cinnamon sticks (optional)

Cut each squash in half crosswise; remove and discard seeds. Place squash halves, cut sides down, in a 15- x 10- x 1-inch jellyroll pan lightly coated with cooking spray. Bake, uncovered, at 350° for 35 minutes.

Turn squash halves over. Combine pineapple, orange, and brown sugar; spoon evenly into squash halves. Sprinkle with ground cinnamon. Bake, uncovered, 10 to 15 additional minutes or until fruit mixture is thoroughly heated. If desired, garnish with orange rind curls and cinnamon sticks. Yield: 4 servings.

PER SERVING: 167 CALORIES (2% FROM FAT)
FAT 0.4G (SATURATED FAT 0.1G)
PROTEIN 2.4G   CARBOHYDRATE 43.1G
CHOLESTEROL 0MG   SODIUM 10MG

Fruited Acorn Squash

HOLIDAY RICE PILAF

When the oven is jam-packed with your holiday fixings, this stovetop pilaf will be a perfect side dish.

1 tablespoon stick margarine
3 cups sliced fresh mushrooms (about 8 ounces)
1 cup chopped sweet red pepper
¾ cup sliced green onions
2 cloves garlic, minced
½ teaspoon salt
3 (10½-ounce) cans low-sodium chicken broth
1 (12-ounce) package wild rice blend
⅓ cup chopped pecans, toasted

Melt margarine in a large nonstick skillet over medium-high heat. Add mushrooms and next 3 ingredients; sauté 5 minutes or until vegetables are tender. Set aside, and keep warm.

Combine salt and broth in a large saucepan; bring to a boil. Add rice blend; cover, reduce heat, and simmer 25 minutes until liquid is absorbed and rice is tender. Stir in mushroom mixture; cook 1 minute or until thoroughly heated. Stir in pecans. Yield: 14 (½-cup) servings.

PER SERVING: 121 CALORIES (23% FROM FAT)
FAT 3.1G (SATURATED FAT 0.4G)
PROTEIN 3.6G   CARBOHYDRATE 20.7G
CHOLESTEROL 0MG   SODIUM 232MG

Hopping John

HOPPING JOHN

1¼ cups dried black-eyed peas
5½ cups water
½ teaspoon salt
¼ cup plus 2 tablespoons chopped onion
¼ cup white vinegar
1 tablespoon olive oil
1⅓ cups chopped onion
3 cloves garlic, minced
1 cup long-grain rice, uncooked
1 teaspoon dried oregano
¼ teaspoon hot sauce
⅔ cup diced lower-salt, reduced-fat cooked
    ham (about 3 ounces)

Sort and wash peas; place in a Dutch oven. Cover with water to depth of 2 inches above peas; soak overnight. Drain. Return peas to Dutch oven; add 5½ cups water and salt. Bring to a boil. Cover, reduce heat, and simmer 35 minutes.

Combine ¼ cup plus 2 tablespoons chopped onion and vinegar. Let stand 30 minutes; drain.

Heat oil in a small skillet over medium heat. Add 1⅓ cups onion and garlic; sauté 5 minutes or until tender. Remove from heat, and add to peas.

Stir in rice, oregano, and hot sauce; cover and simmer 15 minutes. Stir in ham, and cook 10 additional minutes. Serve with onion-vinegar mixture. Yield: 6 (1-cup) servings.

PER SERVING: 211 CALORIES (15% FROM FAT)
FAT 3.5G (SATURATED FAT 0.7G)
PROTEIN 8.2G   CARBOHYDRATE 36.8G
CHOLESTEROL 7MG   SODIUM 311MG

NEW ENGLAND BREAD STUFFING

12 cups (½-inch) cubed white bread (about
   24 slices)
2 tablespoons stick margarine
1½ cups chopped celery
1 cup chopped onion
2 tablespoons water
1 tablespoon sugar
2½ teaspoons poultry seasoning
¾ teaspoon dried basil
¼ teaspoon salt
¼ teaspoon ground nutmeg
¼ teaspoon pepper
1 cup canned low-sodium chicken broth
1 egg, lightly beaten
Vegetable cooking spray
Fresh parsley sprigs (optional)
Fresh sage sprigs (optional)

Place bread cubes on a 15- x 10- x 1-inch jellyroll pan; bake at 325° for 20 minutes or until toasted. Set aside.

Melt margarine in a large skillet over medium heat. Add celery, onion, and water; cover, reduce heat, and cook 15 minutes or until vegetables are tender. Remove from heat. Stir in sugar and next 5 ingredients.

Combine bread cubes, celery mixture, broth, and egg. Spoon mixture into a 2-quart baking dish coated with cooking spray. Bake, uncovered, at 325° for 35 minutes. If desired, garnish with fresh parsley and sage. Yield: 8 (1-cup) servings.

PER SERVING: 221 CALORIES (24% FROM FAT)
FAT 5.8G (SATURATED FAT 1.3G)
PROTEIN 6.8G CARBOHYDRATE 35.4G
CHOLESTEROL 29MG SODIUM 450MG

FRUIT AND CHEESE BREAD DRESSING

Apples and Cheddar cheese make nice additions to a bread dressing that complements ham or pork.

10 (1-ounce) slices French bread, cut into
   ¾-inch cubes
2 tablespoons stick margarine, melted
½ cup firmly packed brown sugar
1½ teaspoons ground cinnamon
1¼ cups water
6 whole cloves
3 (½-inch-thick) slices orange
3 (¼-inch-thick) slices lemon
4 cups diced unpeeled Rome apple (about 1¼
   pounds)
1 cup (4 ounces) diced Cheddar cheese
⅓ cup raisins
3 tablespoons amaretto
1 egg, lightly beaten
Vegetable cooking spray

Place bread cubes on a 15- x 10- x 1-inch jellyroll pan; drizzle margarine over bread. Bake at 350° for 10 minutes or until toasted; set aside.

Combine brown sugar, cinnamon, and water in a small saucepan; stir well. Add cloves, orange slices, and lemon slices; bring to a boil. Reduce heat, and simmer, uncovered, 5 minutes. Strain through a sieve into a large bowl; discard solids. Add bread cubes, apple, and next 4 ingredients; stir well.

Spoon mixture into a 13- x 9- x 2-inch baking dish coated with cooking spray. Bake at 350° for 45 minutes. Yield: 9 (1-cup) servings.

PER SERVING: 273 CALORIES (27% FROM FAT)
FAT 8.2G (SATURATED FAT 3.6G)
PROTEIN 7.0G CARBOHYDRATE 43.5G
CHOLESTEROL 38MG SODIUM 303MG

Cornbread Dressing

CORNBREAD DRESSING

2 hard-cooked eggs
Basic Cornbread
1 (12-ounce) can refrigerated fluffy buttermilk
    biscuits
1½ teaspoons rubbed sage
½ teaspoon pepper
5 cups canned low-sodium chicken broth
⅔ cup chopped celery
⅔ cup chopped onion
2 eggs whites, lightly beaten
Vegetable cooking spray

Slice hard-cooked eggs in half lengthwise; carefully remove yolks from egg whites. Chop egg whites, and set aside. Reserve egg yolks for another use.

Crumble Basic Cornbread; set aside. Bake biscuits according to package directions; cool. Tear 8 biscuits into small pieces; reserve remaining 2 biscuits for another use. Combine chopped egg white, cornbread, torn biscuits, sage, and pepper.

Bring broth to a boil in a saucepan. Add celery and onion. Reduce heat; simmer, uncovered, 5 minutes. Add broth mixture to cornbread mixture; stir well. Add beaten egg whites; stir well. Spoon mixture into a 2-quart baking dish coated with cooking spray. Bake, uncovered, at 400° for 45 minutes. Yield: 12 (½-cup) servings.

BASIC CORNBREAD

1 cup yellow cornmeal
1 cup all-purpose flour
1 tablespoon baking powder
½ teaspoon salt
1¼ cups fat-free milk
2 egg whites, lightly beaten
Vegetable cooking spray

Combine first 4 ingredients in a large bowl; stir well. Combine milk and egg whites; add to flour mixture, stirring just until dry ingredients are moistened.

Pour batter into a 9-inch square baking pan coated with cooking spray. Bake at 400° for 20 minutes or until a wooden pick inserted in center comes out clean. Remove from pan; cool completely on a wire rack. Yield: 12 servings.

PER SERVING: 180 CALORIES (19% FROM FAT)
FAT 3.8G (SATURATED FAT 0.9G)
PROTEIN 7.1G   CARBOHYDRATE 29.3G
CHOLESTEROL 1MG   SODIUM 391MG

Turkey Gravy

How to Degrease Turkey Drippings

To remove fat from roasted turkey drippings, simply chill the drippings overnight; then lift off the solidified fat. But for a quicker way, place the drippings in a large heavy-duty, zip-top plastic bag (the fat will rise to the top). Carefully snip off one corner of the bag. Begin draining the drippings into a four-cup measure or large bowl, stopping before the fat layer reaches the opening.

TURKEY GRAVY

*Be sure to follow the directions in the box
at left to degrease the drippings.*

1 tablespoon stick margarine
3 tablespoons all-purpose flour
1 cup canned low-sodium chicken broth
1 cup degreased turkey drippings
¼ cup dry white wine
¼ teaspoon salt

Melt margarine in a heavy saucepan over medium heat. Stir in flour, and cook, stirring constantly with a wire whisk, 1 minute. Gradually add chicken broth and remaining ingredients, stirring constantly.

Bring to a boil, stirring constantly. Reduce heat; simmer, uncovered, until slightly thickened. Yield: 7 (⅓-cup) servings.

PER SERVING: 57 CALORIES (44% FROM FAT)
FAT 2.8G (SATURATED FAT 0.6G)
PROTEIN 3.3G   CARBOHYDRATE 3.2G
CHOLESTEROL 6MG   SODIUM 128MG

Sour Cream Pound Cake (recipe on page 107)

CLASSIC DESSERTS

Pecans, pumpkins, cranberries, cinnamon, nutmeg—holiday desserts wouldn't be the same without these ingredients, and the rich recipes throughout this chapter are full of them. Carrot Cake with Cream Cheese Frosting (page 100), Dark Chocolate Soufflé Cake (page 100), and Maple-Pecan Tart (page 108) are just a few of the classics here. Each is sinfully delicious, yet surprisingly low in fat. For a twist on traditional pumpkin pie, try Brandied Pumpkin-Ice Cream Pie with Malted Pecans (page 117).

You'll find so many luscious cakes, tarts, and other desserts, you may even want to throw a holiday dessert party. Just prepare several make-aheads, such as Chocolate Silk Cheesecake (page 102), Cream Cheese-Cranberry Tart (page 110), and Fudgy Mint Brownie Dessert (page 115). Plan this evening celebration for eight o'clock or so, decorate your table with a showy centerpiece, set out the sweets, and have fun!

CARROT CAKE WITH CREAM CHEESE FROSTING

For best results, lightly spoon flour into dry measuring cups, and level with a knife.

Vegetable cooking spray
2¼ cups plus 1 tablespoon all-purpose flour
2 teaspoons baking powder
½ teaspoon salt
¼ teaspoon baking soda
1½ teaspoons ground cinnamon
¼ teaspoon ground nutmeg
⅔ cup sugar
⅔ cup firmly packed dark brown sugar
½ cup unsweetened applesauce
½ cup vegetable oil
¼ cup plain nonfat yogurt
2½ teaspoons vanilla extract
2 egg whites
1 egg
2 cups finely shredded carrot
Cream Cheese Frosting
¼ cup chopped walnuts

Coat two 8-inch round cakepans with cooking spray; dust pans evenly with 1 tablespoon flour.

Combine remaining 2¼ cups flour, baking powder, and next 4 ingredients in a large bowl. Combine ⅔ cup sugar, brown sugar, and next 6 ingredients; beat well at medium speed of an electric mixer. Add to flour mixture, stirring just until dry ingredients are moistened. Stir in carrot.

Pour cake batter into prepared pans. Sharply tap pans once on counter to remove air bubbles. Bake at 375° for 30 minutes or until a wooden pick inserted in center comes out clean. Cool in pans on wire racks 10 minutes; remove from pans. Cool completely on wire racks.

Place 1 cake layer on a serving plate; spread with ⅔ cup Cream Cheese Frosting, and top with remaining cake layer. Spread remaining frosting over top and sides of cake. Sprinkle walnuts over cake. Store loosely covered in refrigerator. Yield: 16 servings.

CREAM CHEESE FROSTING
⅔ cup tub-style light cream cheese, chilled
1¼ teaspoons vanilla extract
3½ cups sifted powdered sugar

Beat cream cheese and vanilla in a large bowl at medium speed of an electric mixer until smooth. Gradually add sugar; beat at low speed until smooth (do not overbeat). Cover and chill. Yield: 1⅔ cups.

PER SERVING: 329 CALORIES (21% FROM FAT)
FAT 7.8G (SATURATED FAT 2.0G)
PROTEIN 4.5G   CARBOHYDRATE 61.1G
CHOLESTEROL 19MG   SODIUM 219MG

DARK CHOCOLATE SOUFFLÉ CAKE

Cake flour is a fine-textured, soft wheat flour with a high starch content, and usually comes in a box rather than a bag. You will find it with cake mixes at the supermarket.

Vegetable cooking spray
½ cup sugar
½ cup firmly packed dark brown sugar
¾ cup water
1 tablespoon instant espresso powder or 2 tablespoons instant coffee granules
⅔ cup Dutch process or unsweetened cocoa
¼ teaspoon salt
2 ounces semisweet chocolate, chopped
2 ounces unsweetened chocolate, chopped
2 tablespoons Kahlúa or other coffee-flavored liqueur
3 egg yolks
⅓ cup sifted cake flour
6 egg whites
¼ teaspoon cream of tartar
⅓ cup sugar
1 tablespoon powdered sugar
Fresh raspberries (optional)
Chocolate curls (optional)

Dark Chocolate Soufflé Cake

Coat bottom of a 9-inch springform pan with cooking spray. Set aside.

Combine ½ cup sugar, brown sugar, water, and espresso powder in a large saucepan; stir well. Bring to a boil. Remove from heat; add cocoa and next 3 ingredients, stirring with a wire whisk until chocolates melt. Stir in Kahlúa and egg yolks. Stir in flour; cool to room temperature. Set aside.

Beat egg whites and cream of tartar at high speed of an electric mixer until foamy. Add ⅓ cup sugar, 1 tablespoon at a time, beating until stiff peaks form. Gently fold one-fourth of egg white mixture into chocolate mixture; repeat procedure with remaining egg white mixture, one-fourth at a time. Spoon into prepared pan.

Bake at 300° for 1 hour or until a wooden pick inserted in center comes out almost clean. Cool completely on wire rack. Remove sides from pan; sift powdered sugar over cake. If desired, garnish with fresh raspberries and chocolate curls. Yield: 12 servings.

PER SERVING: 205 CALORIES (27% FROM FAT)
FAT 6.1G (SATURATED FAT 3.2G)
PROTEIN 5.0G CARBOHYDRATE 34.2G
CHOLESTEROL 55MG SODIUM 91MG

CHOCOLATE SILK CHEESECAKE

⅔ cup reduced-calorie chocolate wafer crumbs
   (about 20 cookies)
2 tablespoons sugar
1 tablespoon stick margarine, melted
1 tablespoon water
Vegetable cooking spray
3 ounces semisweet chocolate, chopped
2 tablespoons fat-free milk
1¼ cups sugar
1 tablespoon vanilla extract
¼ teaspoon salt
3 (8-ounce) blocks nonfat cream cheese
1 (8-ounce) block ⅓-less-fat cream cheese
4 egg whites
½ cup Dutch process or unsweetened cocoa
½ cup hot fudge topping
1 cup low-fat sour cream

Combine first 4 ingredients; toss with a fork until blended. Press crumb mixture into bottom of a 9-inch springform pan coated with cooking spray. Bake at 400° for 8 minutes. Cool crust on a wire rack. Increase oven temperature to 525°.

Combine chocolate and milk in a microwave-safe bowl; microwave at high 45 seconds or until chocolate melts, stirring after 30 seconds. Cool.

Position knife blade in food processor bowl; add 1¼ cups sugar and next 4 ingredients. Process just until smooth. Add egg whites, and process until blended. Add chocolate mixture, cocoa, fudge topping, and sour cream; process until blended.

Spoon batter into prepared crust. Bake at 525° for 7 minutes. Reduce oven temperature to 250° (do not remove pan from oven); bake 25 minutes or until almost set. Cheesecake is done when center barely moves when pan is touched. Remove cheesecake from oven; run a knife around outside edge, and cool to room temperature. Cover and chill at least 8 hours. Yield: 16 servings.

PER SERVING: 261 CALORIES (30% FROM FAT)
FAT 8.6G (SATURATED FAT 4.7G)
PROTEIN 11.0G CARBOHYDRATE 35.8G
CHOLESTEROL 26MG SODIUM 455MG

CINNAMON-APPLE CAKE

This cake is usually served during Hanukkah. Cream cheese in the batter gives the cake lots of moisture. Because it's so tender, use a serrated knife for cutting.

1½ cups sugar
½ cup stick margarine, softened
1 teaspoon vanilla extract
6 ounces block-style nonfat cream cheese,
   softened
2 eggs
1½ cups all-purpose flour
1½ teaspoons baking powder
¼ teaspoon salt
¼ cup sugar
2 teaspoons ground cinnamon
3 cups peeled, chopped Rome apple
Vegetable cooking spray

Beat first 4 ingredients at medium speed of an electric mixer until well blended (about 4 minutes). Add eggs, one at a time, beating well after each addition. Combine flour, baking powder, and salt; add to margarine mixture, beating at low speed until blended.

Combine ¼ cup sugar and cinnamon. Combine 2 tablespoons cinnamon mixture and apple; stir apple mixture into batter. Pour batter into an 8-inch springform pan coated with cooking spray; sprinkle with remaining cinnamon mixture.

Bake at 350° for 1 hour and 15 minutes or until cake pulls away from sides of pan. Cool cake completely on a wire rack; cut using a serrated knife. Yield: 12 servings.

Note: You can also make this cake in a 9-inch square cakepan or a 9-inch springform pan; just reduce cooking time by 5 minutes.

PER SERVING: 281 CALORIES (28% FROM FAT)
FAT 8.7G (SATURATED FAT 1.8G)
PROTEIN 4.8G CARBOHYDRATE 46.3G
CHOLESTEROL 39MG SODIUM 284MG

Cinnamon-Apple Cake

CRANBERRY UPSIDE-DOWN CAKE

1 tablespoon stick margarine, melted
½ cup firmly packed brown sugar
2 cups fresh or frozen cranberries, thawed
¼ cup stick margarine, softened
1 cup sugar
2 eggs
1½ teaspoons vanilla extract
1½ cups sifted cake flour
1½ teaspoons baking powder
1 teaspoon ground cinnamon
¾ cup low-fat buttermilk

Pour 1 tablespoon melted margarine into a 9-inch springform pan. Combine brown sugar and cranberries; arrange in a single layer over melted margarine.

Beat ¼ cup margarine and 1 cup sugar at medium speed of an electric mixer until well blended. Add eggs, one at time, beating well after each addition; add vanilla. Combine flour, baking powder, and cinnamon, stirring well; add to creamed mixture alternately with buttermilk, beginning and ending with flour mixture.

Spoon batter evenly over cranberries. Bake at 350° for 45 minutes or until a wooden pick inserted in center comes out clean. Invert cake onto a serving platter. Yield: 8 servings.

PER SERVING: 314 CALORIES (26% FROM FAT)
FAT 9.0G (SATURATED FAT 2.1G)
PROTEIN 4.3G CARBOHYDRATE 54.7G
CHOLESTEROL 55MG SODIUM 191MG

PUMPKIN-SPICE BUNDT CAKE

The rum glaze will seep into the cake if you spoon it on while the cake is still warm.

3¼ cups all-purpose flour
1 tablespoon baking powder
1 teaspoon baking soda
¼ teaspoon salt
2½ teaspoons ground cinnamon
1 teaspoon ground nutmeg
1½ cups fresh or canned pumpkin puree
½ cup unsweetened applesauce
1½ cups sugar
½ cup stick margarine, softened
3 egg whites
2 teaspoons vanilla extract
Vegetable cooking spray
3 tablespoons dark or light brown sugar
1 tablespoon dark rum
1 teaspoon fat-free milk
3 tablespoons powdered sugar

Combine first 6 ingredients; set aside. Combine pumpkin and applesauce; set aside.

Beat 1½ cups sugar and margarine in a large bowl at medium speed of an electric mixer until well blended (about 5 minutes). Add egg whites and vanilla, beating well. Add flour mixture to sugar mixture alternately with pumpkin mixture, beginning and ending with flour mixture.

Pour batter into a 12-cup Bundt pan coated with cooking spray. Bake at 350° for 50 minutes or until a wooden pick inserted in center comes out clean. Cool in pan 10 minutes; remove from pan.

Combine brown sugar, rum, and milk in a small saucepan; cook over low heat until brown sugar dissolves. Remove from heat, and add powdered sugar, stirring with a wire whisk. Spoon glaze over warm cake. Yield: 16 servings.

PER SERVING: 248 CALORIES (22% FROM FAT)
FAT 6.1G (SATURATED FAT 1.2G)
PROTEIN 3.7G CARBOHYDRATE 44.8G
CHOLESTEROL 0MG SODIUM 269MG

ZUCCHINI-STREUSEL BUNDT CAKE

2 cups coarsely shredded zucchini
⅓ cup firmly packed brown sugar
⅓ cup chopped walnuts
⅓ cup currants
1 tablespoon ground cinnamon
½ teaspoon ground allspice
3 cups all-purpose flour
1½ teaspoons baking powder
1 teaspoon baking soda
½ teaspoon salt
1¼ cups sugar
1⅓ cups plain nonfat yogurt
⅓ cup vegetable oil
1 tablespoon vanilla extract
2 egg whites, lightly beaten
1 egg, lightly beaten
Vegetable cooking spray
1 tablespoon fine, dry breadcrumbs
¾ cup sifted powdered sugar
2 teaspoons fat-free milk
1 teaspoon vanilla extract

Place zucchini on layers of paper towels; cover with additional paper towels. Let stand 5 minutes; set zucchini aside. Combine brown sugar and next 4 ingredients in a bowl; stir well, and set aside.

Combine flour and next 4 ingredients in a bowl; make a well in center. Combine yogurt and next 4 ingredients, stirring well; add zucchini. Add yogurt mixture to flour mixture, stirring just until moistened.

Coat a 12-cup Bundt pan with cooking spray; sprinkle with breadcrumbs. Spoon one-third of batter into pan; top with half of brown sugar mixture. Spoon half of remaining batter into pan; top with remaining brown sugar mixture and batter.

Bake at 350° for 1 hour or until a wooden pick inserted comes out clean. Cool in pan on a wire rack 10 minutes; remove from pan. Cool completely on wire rack. Combine powdered sugar, milk, and vanilla; drizzle glaze over cake. Yield: 18 servings.

PER SERVING: 245 CALORIES (22% FROM FAT)
FAT 6.0G (SATURATED FAT 1.0G)
PROTEIN 4.8G CARBOHYDRATE 43.5G
CHOLESTEROL 13MG SODIUM 164MG

Zucchini-Streusel Bundt Cake

Holiday Cake with Dried Fruit

HOLIDAY CAKE WITH DRIED FRUIT

Vegetable cooking spray
3 cups all-purpose flour
½ cup cornstarch
¼ teaspoon salt
½ cup chopped dried peaches
½ cup chopped dried dates
½ cup chopped dried pears
½ cup dried cranberries
½ cup dried sour cherries
2 cups sugar
½ cup stick margarine, softened
1 (8-ounce) block ⅓-less-fat cream cheese
1 tablespoon grated lemon rind
1 tablespoon vanilla extract
4 eggs
2 egg whites
1 cup nonfat sour cream
1 teaspoon baking soda
1 tablespoon powdered sugar
Lemon rind curls (optional)
Canned dark sweet cherries (optional)

Coat a 12-cup Bundt pan with cooking spray, and set aside.

Sift together flour, cornstarch, and salt twice. Combine ¼ cup flour mixture, dried peaches, and next 4 ingredients, tossing to coat. Set aside remaining flour mixture.

Combine sugar and next 4 ingredients in a bowl; beat at medium speed of an electric mixer until well blended (about 5 minutes). Add eggs and egg whites, one at a time, beating well after each addition.

Combine sour cream and baking soda, stirring well. Add reserved flour mixture to sugar mixture alternately with sour cream mixture, beginning and ending with flour mixture. Mix well after each addition. Gently fold in dried fruit mixture.

Pour batter into prepared pan. Bake at 350° for 1 hour or until wooden pick inserted in center comes out clean. Cool cake in pan on a wire rack 10 minutes; remove from pan. Cool completely on wire rack. Dust cake with powdered sugar. If desired, garnish with lemon rind curls and sweet cherries. Yield: 24 servings.

Note: Substitute two 8-ounce bags dried mixed fruit for peaches, dates, pears, cranberries, and cherries, if desired.

PER SERVING: 259 CALORIES (25% FROM FAT)
FAT 7.1G (SATURATED FAT 2.5G)
PROTEIN 5.1G CARBOHYDRATE 44.4G
CHOLESTEROL 44MG SODIUM 183MG

SOUR CREAM POUND CAKE

(pictured on page 98)

Although this adaptation of a favorite recipe cuts the fat content in half and cholesterol even more, the cake remains tender and moist.

3 cups sugar
¾ cup stick margarine, softened
1⅓ cups fat-free egg substitute
1½ cups low-fat sour cream
1 teaspoon baking soda
4½ cups sifted cake flour
¼ teaspoon salt
2 teaspoons vanilla extract
Vegetable cooking spray
Cranberries (optional)

Beat sugar and margarine at medium speed of an electric mixer until well blended (about 5 minutes). Add egg substitute; beat well. Combine sour cream and baking soda; stir well. Combine flour and salt; add to margarine mixture alternately with sour cream mixture, beginning and ending with flour mixture. Stir in vanilla. Pour batter into a 10-inch tube pan coated with cooking spray. Bake at 325° for 1 hour and 35 minutes or until a wooden pick inserted in center comes out clean. Cool in pan 10 minutes; remove from pan. Cool on a wire rack. Garnish with cranberries, if desired. Yield: 24 servings.

Note: Use 8 egg whites in place of egg substitute, if desired, adding one at a time to sugar mixture.

PER SERVING: 250 CALORIES (28% FROM FAT)
FAT 7.7G (SATURATED FAT 2.3G)
PROTEIN 3.5G CARBOHYDRATE 41.9G
CHOLESTEROL 6MG SODIUM 170MG

DOUBLE-CHOCOLATE CREAM TART

1 cup all-purpose flour, divided
¼ cup ice water
1 tablespoon vanilla extract, divided
¾ cup unsweetened cocoa, divided
2 tablespoons sugar
¼ teaspoon salt
¼ cup shortening
Vegetable cooking spray
1 (14-ounce) can fat-free sweetened condensed
    milk
6 ounces block-style ⅓-less-fat cream cheese,
    softened
1 egg
1 egg white
1½ cups frozen reduced-calorie whipped
    topping, thawed
1 ounce semisweet chocolate, finely chopped

Combine ¼ cup flour, ice water, and 1 teaspoon vanilla, stirring until well blended; set aside.

Combine remaining ¾ cup flour, ¼ cup cocoa, sugar, and salt in a bowl; cut in shortening until mixture resembles coarse meal. Add ice water mixture; toss with a fork until dry ingredients are moistened and mixture is crumbly (do not form a ball).

Gently press mixture into a 4-inch circle on heavy-duty plastic wrap; cover with additional plastic wrap. Roll dough, still covered, into a 13-inch circle. Place dough in freezer 30 minutes or until plastic wrap can be removed easily.

Remove top sheet of plastic wrap; fit dough, uncovered side down, into a 10-inch round removable-bottom tart pan coated with cooking spray. Remove remaining sheet of plastic wrap. Fold edges under; flute. Pierce bottom and sides of dough with a fork; bake at 350° for 4 minutes. Cool on a wire rack. Place pan on a baking sheet; set aside.

Beat remaining ½ cup cocoa and milk at medium speed of an electric mixer until blended. Add cream cheese; beat well. Add remaining 2 teaspoons vanilla, egg, and egg white; beat just until smooth. Pour mixture into crust; bake at 350° for 25 minutes or until set. (Do not overbake.) Cool completely on a wire rack.

Spread whipped topping over tart; sprinkle with chopped chocolate. Yield: 12 servings.

PER SERVING: 266 CALORIES (33% FROM FAT)
FAT 9.7G (SATURATED FAT 3.8G)
PROTEIN 7.8G CARBOHYDRATE 36.1G
CHOLESTEROL 32MG SODIUM 161MG

MAPLE-PECAN TART

1 cup all-purpose flour, divided
3½ tablespoons ice water
1 teaspoon sugar
¼ teaspoon salt
3 tablespoons shortening
Vegetable cooking spray
1 cup low-fat granola (without raisins)
1 cup maple syrup
2 teaspoons vanilla extract
⅛ teaspoon salt
3 egg whites
1 egg
⅓ cup chopped pecans

Combine ¼ cup flour and ice water, stirring with a wire whisk until well blended; set aside.

Combine remaining ¾ cup flour, sugar, and ¼ teaspoon salt in a bowl; cut in shortening until mixture resembles coarse meal. Add ice water mixture, and toss with a fork just until moistened. Press mixture into a 4-inch circle on heavy-duty plastic wrap; cover with additional plastic wrap. Chill 30 minutes.

Roll dough, still covered, into an 11-inch circle. Remove top sheet of plastic wrap; fit dough, uncovered side down, into a 9-inch round tart pan coated with cooking spray. Remove remaining plastic wrap.

Sprinkle granola into pastry shell. Combine syrup and next 4 ingredients. Stir well with whisk; pour into pastry shell. Sprinkle with pecans.

Place tart pan on a baking sheet; bake at 450° for 10 minutes. Reduce heat to 325° (do not remove pan from oven); bake 20 minutes or until filling is set. Cool on a wire rack. Yield: 8 servings.

PER SERVING: 286 CALORIES (28% FROM FAT)
FAT 8.9G (SATURATED FAT 1.5G)
PROTEIN 4.7G CARBOHYDRATE 48.0G
CHOLESTEROL 27MG SODIUM 155MG

Maple-Pecan Tart

Cream Cheese-Cranberry Tart

CREAM CHEESE-CRANBERRY TART

1¼ cups all-purpose flour
⅛ teaspoon salt
¼ cup chilled stick margarine, cut into
     4 pieces
2 to 3 tablespoons ice water
Vegetable cooking spray
⅔ cup 1% low-fat cottage cheese
⅓ cup tub-style light process cream cheese
¼ cup sugar
1 egg
3 cups fresh cranberries
⅔ cup sugar
¼ cup water
1 tablespoon cornstarch
1 teaspoon grated orange rind
2 tablespoons unsweetened orange juice
Fresh kumquats (optional)

Position knife blade in food processor bowl; add flour and salt. Pulse 2 or 3 times until combined.

Add margarine; pulse 6 to 8 times or until mixture resembles coarse meal. With processor running, slowly add ice water through food chute, processing just until combined. (Do not form a ball.)

Press mixture into a 4-inch circle on heavy-duty plastic wrap; cover with additional plastic wrap. Roll dough, still covered, into a 12-inch circle; freeze 5 minutes or until plastic wrap can be removed easily. Remove top sheet of plastic wrap; fit dough, uncovered side down, into an 11-inch round tart pan coated with cooking spray. Remove remaining sheet of plastic wrap. Prick bottom of pastry with a fork. Bake at 375° for 15 minutes; cool completely on a wire rack.

Place cottage cheese in container of an electric blender; cover and process until smooth. Add cream cheese, ¼ cup sugar, and egg; cover and process until smooth. Pour into prepared crust. Bake at 350° for 20 minutes or until a knife inserted near center comes out clean. Cool on wire rack.

Combine cranberries and next 5 ingredients in saucepan; stir. Bring to a boil; boil, stirring constantly, 1 minute. Remove from heat, and cool; spoon over cream cheese filling. Cover; chill. Garnish with kumquats, if desired. Yield: 12 servings.

PER SERVING: 185 CALORIES (27% FROM FAT)
FAT 5.6G (SATURATED FAT 1.6G)
PROTEIN 4.2G CARBOHYDRATE 30.0G
CHOLESTEROL 23MG SODIUM 162MG

LEMON CREAM TART

1 egg white
2 tablespoons stick margarine, softened
3 tablespoons sugar
3 cups reduced-fat vanilla wafer crumbs
Vegetable cooking spray
3 eggs
1 (14-ounce) can low-fat sweetened condensed
     milk
1 tablespoon grated lemon rind
½ cup fresh lemon juice
1 cup frozen reduced-calorie whipped topping,
     thawed
10 lemon rind strips (optional)
Mint leaves (optional)

Combine first 3 ingredients; beat at high speed of an electric mixer until blended. Add wafer crumbs; toss with a fork until moistened.

Press crumb mixture into bottom and up sides of a 9-inch round tart pan coated with cooking spray. Bake at 325° for 15 minutes or until lightly browned. Cool on a wire rack.

Combine eggs, milk, and lemon rind, stirring well; gradually add lemon juice, stirring with a wire whisk until blended. Pour mixture into prepared crust. Bake at 325° for 30 minutes or until filling is set. Cool completely. Dollop whipped topping around edge of tart. If desired, garnish with lemon rind strips and mint. Yield: 10 servings.

PER SERVING: 256 CALORIES (27% FROM FAT)
FAT 7.8G (SATURATED FAT 2.7G)
PROTEIN 6.5G   CARBOHYDRATE 41.0G
CHOLESTEROL 71MG   SODIUM 159MG

Lemon Cream Tart

PUMPKIN CRÈME BRÛLÉE TART

1 cup all-purpose flour, divided
3½ tablespoons ice water
1 teaspoon sugar
¼ teaspoon salt
3 tablespoons shortening
Vegetable cooking spray
1 cup unsweetened canned pumpkin
1 cup milk
⅓ cup sugar
½ teaspoon pumpkin pie spice
¾ teaspoon vanilla extract
¼ teaspoon butter-flavored extract
Dash of salt
2 eggs, lightly beaten
2 egg whites, lightly beaten
¼ cup firmly packed brown sugar

Combine ¼ cup flour and ice water, stirring with a wire whisk until well blended; set aside. Combine remaining ¾ cup flour, sugar, and ¼ teaspoon salt in a bowl; cut in shortening with a pastry blender until mixture resembles coarse meal. Add ice water mixture; stir with a fork just until dry ingredients are moistened.

Press mixture into a 4-inch circle on heavy-duty plastic wrap; cover with additional plastic wrap. Roll dough, still covered, into an 11-inch circle; chill 10 minutes. Remove top sheet of plastic wrap; fit dough, uncovered side down, into a 10-inch round tart pan coated with cooking spray. Remove remaining sheet of wrap. Prick bottom and sides of dough with a fork; bake at 400° for 15 minutes. Cool on a wire rack.

Combine pumpkin and next 8 ingredients; stir well with whisk. Pour into crust; bake at 350° for 40 minutes or until filling is almost set. Cool on wire rack 30 minutes. Cover loosely; chill at least 4 hours.

Uncover tart. Press brown sugar through a small wire sieve onto filling. Shield edges of piecrust with aluminum foil; broil 1 minute or until sugar is bubbly. Serve immediately. Yield: 8 servings.

PER SERVING: 207 CALORIES (29% FROM FAT)
FAT 6.6G (SATURATED FAT 2.3G)
PROTEIN 5.4G   CARBOHYDRATE 31.4G
CHOLESTEROL 60MG   SODIUM 125MG

Almond Crème Caramel

ALMOND CRÈME CARAMEL

½ cup sugar
4 eggs
1 teaspoon vanilla extract
½ teaspoon almond extract
1 (14-ounce) can fat-free sweetened condensed
   milk
1 (12-ounce) can evaporated skimmed milk
¼ cup coarsely chopped almonds
Chopped almonds (optional)

Pour sugar into a 9-inch round cakepan; cook over medium heat 6 minutes or until sugar dissolves and is golden, shaking pan occasionally with tongs. Immediately remove from heat; set aside.

Beat eggs in a medium bowl with a wire whisk until foamy. Add vanilla and next 3 ingredients, stirring with whisk; stir in ¼ cup almonds. Pour into prepared cakepan; cover with aluminum foil, and place in a large shallow ovenproof pan. Place pan in oven; add water to large pan to a depth of 1 inch. (Aluminum foil should not touch water.) Bake at 350° for 55 minutes or until a knife inserted in center comes out clean.

Remove cakepan from water; place on a wire rack. Remove foil. Cool custard in cakepan 30 minutes. Loosen edges with a knife. Place a serving plate upside down on cakepan; invert onto plate, allowing syrup to drizzle over custard. Sprinkle with chopped almonds, if desired. Yield: 9 servings.

PER SERVING: 253 CALORIES (15% FROM FAT)
FAT 4.3G (SATURATED FAT 0.9G)
PROTEIN 9.8G   CARBOHYDRATE 43.1G
CHOLESTEROL 100MG   SODIUM 118MG

BITTERSWEET CHOCOLATE PUDDING

3½ cups fat-free milk, divided
1 cup Dutch process or unsweetened cocoa
3 tablespoons cornstarch
¼ teaspoon salt
1 cup sugar
1 egg, lightly beaten
1 egg yolk, lightly beaten
2 ounces bittersweet chocolate, coarsely
   chopped
1 tablespoon vanilla extract

Combine 1 cup milk, cocoa, cornstarch, and salt in a large bowl; stir well with a wire whisk.

Cook remaining 2½ cups milk in a large, heavy saucepan over medium-high heat to 180° or until tiny bubbles form around edge (do not boil). Remove from heat; stir in sugar with whisk until sugar dissolves. Add cocoa mixture to pan, stirring until blended. Bring to a boil over medium heat; cook, stirring constantly, 2 minutes.

Combine egg and egg yolk, stirring well with whisk. Gradually add milk mixture to egg mixture, stirring constantly. Return mixture to pan. Cook over medium heat, stirring constantly, until thickened (about 2 minutes). Remove from heat. Stir in chocolate and vanilla; stir until chocolate melts. Serve warm or chilled. Yield: 8 (½-cup) servings.

PER SERVING: 249 CALORIES (18% FROM FAT)
FAT 5.1G (SATURATED FAT 2.7G)
PROTEIN 8.3G   CARBOHYDRATE 43.0G
CHOLESTEROL 57MG   SODIUM 144MG

BLACK BOTTOM CRANBERRY PUDDING

⅔ cup chocolate wafer crumbs
2 tablespoons reduced-calorie stick margarine, melted
¾ cup sugar, divided
¼ cup plus 2 tablespoons water
2 cups frozen cranberries, thawed
¼ cup seedless raspberry jam
1 cup low-fat milk
2 egg yolks
¼ cup all-purpose flour
5 egg whites
1 teaspoon powdered sugar

Combine wafer crumbs and margarine, stirring well. Press crumb mixture into bottom of an 8-inch square pan; set aside.

Combine ¼ cup plus 2 tablespoons sugar and water in a saucepan. Bring to a boil over medium heat. Add cranberries, and return mixture to a boil. Reduce heat; simmer, uncovered, 10 minutes, stirring occasionally. Remove from heat; stir in jam. Cool. Spoon cranberry mixture into prepared crust.

Place milk in a small saucepan; bring just to a boil over medium heat, stirring occasionally. Beat egg yolks and ¼ cup sugar at high speed of an electric mixer until yolks are thick and pale (about 5 minutes). Gently fold flour into yolk mixture, using a large wire whisk. Gradually stir about ¼ cup hot milk into yolk mixture; add to remaining hot milk, stirring constantly. Cook mixture over medium-low heat, stirring constantly, 1 minute or until thickened. Transfer to a large bowl; cool.

Beat egg whites at high speed of mixer until soft peaks form. Gradually add remaining 2 tablespoons sugar, beating until stiff peaks form. Fold one-fourth of beaten egg white mixture into milk mixture; fold in remaining egg white mixture. Pour egg white mixture over cranberry mixture in pan. Bake at 375° for 20 minutes or until puffed and golden. Sprinkle with powdered sugar. Yield: 8 servings.

PER SERVING: 210 CALORIES (23% FROM FAT)
FAT 5.3G (SATURATED FAT 1.3G)
PROTEIN 4.9G   CARBOHYDRATE 36.4G
CHOLESTEROL 62MG   SODIUM 113MG

CREAMY CITRUS TRIFLE

Instant pudding mix is a quick alternative to custard filling in layered desserts such as trifle.

1 (3.4-ounce) package lemon instant pudding mix
2 cups fat-free milk
1 (8-ounce) carton low-fat sour cream
⅓ cup low-sugar orange marmalade
1 tablespoon dry sherry
8 ounces angel food cake, cut into ¾-inch cubes
2 (11-ounce) cans mandarin oranges in light syrup, drained

Combine pudding mix and milk, stirring until smooth. Stir in sour cream; set aside. Combine marmalade and sherry, stirring with a wire whisk until blended.

Arrange half of cake cubes in a 1½-quart trifle bowl or straight-sided glass bowl. Spoon half of pudding mixture over cake. Drizzle marmalade mixture over pudding mixture. Arrange half of oranges over marmalade mixture. Repeat layers. Cover and chill at least 3 hours. Yield: 8 servings.

PER SERVING: 197 CALORIES (16% FROM FAT)
FAT 3.6G (SATURATED FAT 2.2G)
PROTEIN 4.7G   CARBOHYDRATE 37.2G
CHOLESTEROL 12MG   SODIUM 341MG

FYI

Desserts that contain fresh fruit, pudding, or milk products should be stored in the refrigerator both before and after serving. If the recipe doesn't specify freezing, it's probably not a good candidate to be made ahead and frozen. Freezing changes the texture of most fruit dishes, and pudding-based recipes have a tendency to break down. Turn to pages 117 and 118 for several freezer-friendly recipes.

Tiramisù

TIRAMISÙ

Tiramisù is an Italian dessert with layers of coffee liqueur-soaked spongecake, mascarpone (a sweet cream cheese), and chocolate.

½ cup plus 1 tablespoon Kahlúa or other
   coffee-flavored liqueur
¼ cup plus 1 tablespoon sugar, divided
2 tablespoons water
1 tablespoon plus 1 teaspoon instant espresso
   powder
¼ cup plus 2 tablespoons liquid fat-free
   hazelnut-flavored nondairy coffee creamer
1 cup tub-style light process cream cheese,
   softened
1½ cups frozen reduced-calorie whipped
   topping, thawed
1 (13.6-ounce) loaf fat-free pound cake, cut
   into 16 slices
Unsweetened cocoa (optional)

Combine Kahlúa, 1 tablespoon sugar, water, and espresso powder, stirring until sugar and espresso powder dissolve. Spoon 2 tablespoons mixture into a medium bowl; set remaining mixture aside.

Add remaining ¼ cup sugar and creamer to 2 tablespoons liqueur mixture in bowl, stirring until sugar dissolves. Add cream cheese; beat at medium speed of an electric mixer until smooth. Fold in whipped topping.

Place 1 cake slice in each of eight wine glasses or eight 4-ounce custard cups. Brush cake in glasses generously with half of reserved liqueur mixture. Spread cheese mixture evenly over cake. Top with remaining 8 cake slices. Gently press slices into glasses. Brush cake with remaining liqueur mixture. Sprinkle evenly with cocoa, if desired. Serve immediately. Yield: 8 servings.

PER SERVING: 323 CALORIES (18% FROM FAT)
FAT 6.4G (SATURATED FAT 3.7G)
PROTEIN 6.3G   CARBOHYDRATE 50.3G
CHOLESTEROL 16MG   SODIUM 924MG

FUDGY MINT BROWNIE DESSERT

(pictured on cover)

1¼ cups sugar
½ cup fat-free egg substitute
¼ cup stick margarine, melted
2 tablespoons water
1 teaspoon vanilla extract
1¼ cups sifted cake flour
1 teaspoon baking powder
⅛ teaspoon salt
¼ cup plus 2 tablespoons unsweetened cocoa
Vegetable cooking spray
½ cup fat-free hot fudge topping
1 tablespoon crème de menthe
2 cups frozen reduced-calorie whipped
   topping, thawed
¼ cup mint-flavored semisweet chocolate
   morsels, finely chopped
Chocolate-covered mint wafer candy shavings
   (optional)
Fresh mint sprigs (optional)
Fresh raspberries (optional)

Combine first 5 ingredients, stirring well. Combine flour and next 3 ingredients; add to sugar mixture, stirring well. Spoon batter into a 9-inch springform pan coated with cooking spray. Bake at 325° for 25 to 30 minutes or until a wooden pick inserted in center comes out clean. Cool slightly on a wire rack.

Combine hot fudge topping and crème de menthe in a small saucepan; cook over low heat until heated, stirring often. Cool slightly. Prick brownie several times with a fork or wooden pick. Pour warm fudge mixture over brownie. Cool completely.

Combine whipped topping and chocolate morsels; spread over brownie. Cover and chill. Cut into wedges. If desired, garnish with candy shavings, mint sprigs, and raspberries. Yield: 12 servings.

Note: To make candy shavings, pull a vegetable peeler down narrow sides of a chocolate-flavored mint wafer candy, such as Andes Mints.

PER SERVING: 249 CALORIES (25% FROM FAT)
FAT 6.9G (SATURATED FAT 2.7G)
PROTEIN 3.9G   CARBOHYDRATE 44.0G
CHOLESTEROL 0MG   SODIUM 159MG

CITRUS AND DRIED FRUIT COMPOTE

1 cup water
⅔ cup sugar
¾ cup dried apricot halves
⅓ cup dried tart cherries
¼ cup golden raisins
2 cups pink grapefruit sections (about
    2 large grapefruit)
2 cups orange sections (about 3 large
    oranges)
1 teaspoon chopped fresh mint
Fresh mint sprigs (optional)

Combine water and sugar in a saucepan; bring to a boil. Add apricots, cherries, and raisins; stir well. Cover, reduce heat, and simmer 10 minutes. Pour mixture into a bowl; cool. Stir in grapefruit, orange, and chopped mint. Serve chilled or at room temperature. Garnish with mint sprigs, if desired. Yield: 10 (½-cup) servings.

PER SERVING: 143 CALORIES (2% FROM FAT)
FAT 0.3G (SATURATED FAT 0.0G)
PROTEIN 1.4G   CARBOHYDRATE 36.8G
CHOLESTEROL 0MG   SODIUM 9MG

Citrus and Dried Fruit Compote

BRANDIED PUMPKIN-ICE CREAM PIE WITH MALTED PECANS

1½ cups graham cracker crumbs
½ teaspoon ground cinnamon
1 tablespoon water
2 egg whites, lightly beaten
Vegetable cooking spray
1 cup unsweetened canned pumpkin
⅓ cup firmly packed brown sugar
1 teaspoon ground cinnamon
¼ teaspoon ground allspice
¼ teaspoon ground nutmeg
⅛ teaspoon ground ginger
2 tablespoons brandy (optional)
4 cups vanilla low-fat ice cream, softened
3 tablespoons chopped pecans, toasted
2 tablespoons malted milk powder

Combine first 4 ingredients; toss with a fork until dry ingredients are moistened. Press onto bottom and up sides of a 9-inch pieplate coated with cooking spray. Bake at 350° for 10 minutes; cool on a wire rack.

Combine pumpkin and next 5 ingredients in a large bowl; stir well. Stir in brandy, if desired. Fold in ice cream to create a marbled effect. Spoon pumpkin mixture into prepared crust. Cover loosely, and freeze 8 hours.

Place pie in refrigerator 20 minutes before serving to soften. Position knife blade in food processor bowl; add pecans and malted milk powder. Process until ground. Sprinkle pecan mixture around edge of pie. Yield: 8 servings.

PER SERVING: 246 CALORIES (26% FROM FAT)
FAT 7.0G (SATURATED FAT 2.4G)
PROTEIN 4.9G   CARBOHYDRATE 42.5G
CHOLESTEROL 10MG   SODIUM 194MG

Brandied Pumpkin-Ice Cream Pie with Malted Pecans

CARAMEL-KAHLÚA SQUARES

¼ cup plus 1 tablespoon chocolate wafer crumbs (about 6 wafers)
2 teaspoons reduced-calorie stick margarine, melted
Vegetable cooking spray
2 tablespoons Kahlúa or other coffee-flavored liqueur
6 cups vanilla low-fat ice cream, softened
½ cup fat-free caramel-flavored syrup
2 tablespoons strongly brewed coffee

Combine wafer crumbs and margarine, stirring well. Sprinkle half of crumb mixture over bottom of an 8-inch square pan coated with cooking spray.

Stir Kahlúa into ice cream. Spread half of ice cream mixture into prepared pan. Combine caramel syrup and coffee; drizzle half of caramel mixture over ice cream mixture in pan. Freeze until firm. Repeat layers. Sprinkle with remaining crumb mixture. Freeze until firm. Yield: 9 squares.

PER SQUARE: 201 CALORIES (23% FROM FAT)
FAT 5.1G (SATURATED FAT 2.5G)
PROTEIN 3.5G   CARBOHYDRATE 34.8G
CHOLESTEROL 15MG   SODIUM 126MG

COFFEE-TOFFEE DESSERT

1 (10¾-ounce) loaf angel food cake
1 tablespoon instant coffee granules
1 tablespoon hot water
1 teaspoon vanilla extract
4 cups vanilla nonfat frozen yogurt,
    softened
4 (1.4-ounce) chocolate-covered toffee candy
    bars, crushed
2 tablespoons Kahlúa or other coffee-flavored
    liqueur
1 (8-ounce) tub frozen reduced-calorie
    whipped topping, thawed

Cut cake into ½-inch slices. Arrange cake slices, overlapping, over bottom of a 9-inch springform pan; set aside.

Combine coffee granules, hot water, and vanilla in a large bowl; stir well. Stir in frozen yogurt and crushed candy bars; spread mixture over cake slices. Gently stir Kahlúa into whipped topping, and spread over frozen yogurt mixture. Cover and freeze 8 hours or until firm. Cut into wedges. Yield: 14 servings.

PER SERVING: 228 CALORIES (24% FROM FAT)
FAT 6.1G (SATURATED FAT 3.9G)
PROTEIN 4.1G CARBOHYDRATE 35.0G
CHOLESTEROL 0MG SODIUM 111MG

CRANBERRY ICE

8 cups water
4 cups fresh cranberries
3 cups sugar

Combine all ingredients in a Dutch oven; bring to a boil. Reduce heat, and cook 15 minutes or until all cranberries pop. Strain cranberry mixture through a fine sieve over a bowl, discarding solids. Cover and chill.

Pour cranberry mixture into freezer container of a 4-quart hand-turned or electric freezer. Freeze according to manufacturer's instructions. Spoon into a freezer-safe container; cover and freeze 1 hour or until ready to serve. Yield: 20 (½-cup) servings.

PER SERVING: 125 CALORIES (0% FROM FAT)
FAT 0.0G (SATURATED FAT 0.0G)
PROTEIN 0.1G CARBOHYDRATE 32.4G
CHOLESTEROL 0MG SODIUM 0MG

FRESH ORANGE SORBET

*To get fresh juice for this sorbet, you'll
need about 10 medium-size oranges and
2 medium-size lemons.*

2½ cups water
1 cup sugar
Orange rind strips from 2 oranges
2⅔ cups fresh orange juice
⅓ cup fresh lemon juice
Orange rind curls (optional)

Combine water and sugar in a small saucepan; bring to a boil. Add orange rind strips; reduce heat, and simmer 5 minutes. Remove and discard orange rind strips. Remove liquid from heat, and cool completely. Stir in orange juice and lemon juice.

Pour mixture into freezer container of a 4-quart hand-turned or electric freezer. Freeze according to manufacturer's instructions. Pack freezer with additional ice and rock salt; let sorbet stand in freezer 1 hour before serving.

Scoop sorbet into individual bowls or dessert dishes. Garnish with orange rind curls, if desired. Serve immediately. Yield: 6 (¾-cup) servings.

PER SERVING: 182 CALORIES (0% FROM FAT)
FAT 0.1G (SATURATED FAT 0.0G)
PROTEIN 0.8G CARBOHYDRATE 46.4G
CHOLESTEROL 0MG SODIUM 11MG

Fresh Orange Sorbet

Frankfurter Brenten (recipe on page 138)

TREATS FROM THE KITCHEN

Often the best holiday gift isn't from a store, but rather from your kitchen. It can be something as simple as a bag of Italian Seasoned Snack Mix (page 124) or as elaborate as a gift basket filled with homemade goodies, such as Curried Peppercorn Mustard (page 123), Potted Herbed Cheese (page 123), and Pickled Sweet Peppers (page 123).

This chapter starts with savory gift recipes, including everything from Marinated Mushrooms (page 122) to Cranberry Wine Vinegar (page 125). Beginning on page 126, you'll find a tempting collection of cookies. Prepare them for giving, sharing with the neighborhood children, or filling your own cookie jar. And be sure to try Apple Spice Minicakes on page 140; pair them with Apple Butter (page 124) for a perfect gift.

Select unique containers for your culinary gifts—they will double the surprise and will be enjoyed long after their edible contents are fond memories. Turn to pages 125 and 137 for creative packaging ideas.

From left: *Marinated Mushrooms, Pickled Sweet Peppers, and Potted Herbed Cheese*

MARINATED MUSHROOMS

1½ pounds medium-size fresh mushrooms
Vegetable cooking spray
2 tablespoons minced garlic
⅓ cup red wine vinegar
1½ tablespoons coriander seeds
¾ teaspoon dried thyme
¾ teaspoon dried oregano
½ teaspoon salt
½ teaspoon freshly ground pepper

Clean mushrooms, and trim stem ends; set mushrooms aside.

Coat a large skillet with cooking spray; place over medium heat until hot. Add garlic; cook 2 minutes. Add vinegar and remaining 5 ingredients; stir mixture well. Add mushrooms. Cover, reduce heat, and simmer 20 minutes or until mushrooms are tender, stirring occasionally. Cool to room temperature. Spoon into airtight containers. Chill 8 hours. Drain before serving. Yield: 6 (½-cup) servings.

PER SERVING: 41 CALORIES (18% FROM FAT)
FAT 0.8G (SATURATED FAT 0.1G)
PROTEIN 2.8G   CARBOHYDRATE 7.8G
CHOLESTEROL 0MG   SODIUM 201MG

PICKLED SWEET PEPPERS

2 large sweet red peppers (about 1 pound)
2 large sweet yellow peppers (about 1 pound)
2 cups water
½ cup sherry vinegar or white wine vinegar
¼ cup honey
1 teaspoon black peppercorns
4 large cloves garlic, thinly sliced
1 cup sliced onion (about 2 small onions)

Cut peppers in half lengthwise; discard seeds and membranes. Cut peppers lengthwise into 1-inch-wide strips.

Combine water and next 4 ingredients in a saucepan; bring to a boil. Add pepper strips and onion; bring to a boil. Cover, reduce heat, and simmer 20 minutes or until pepper strips are very tender. Cool. Store in airtight containers in refrigerator. Serve chilled with a slotted spoon. Yield: 10 (½-cup) servings.

PER SERVING: 52 CALORIES (3% FROM FAT)
FAT 0.2G (SATURATED FAT 0.0G)
PROTEIN 0.5G   CARBOHYDRATE 10.6G
CHOLESTEROL 0MG   SODIUM 73MG

POTTED HERBED CHEESE

1 large clove garlic
¼ cup packed fresh basil leaves
¼ cup chopped green onion tops
1 cup 1% low-fat cottage cheese
½ cup (2 ounces) crumbled feta cheese

Position knife blade in food processor bowl. Drop garlic through food chute with processor running; process 3 seconds or until minced. Add basil and green onion tops; process until finely chopped. Add cheeses; pulse until blended (but still chunky). Chill 8 hours. Serve with crackers or French bread. Store in an airtight container in refrigerator up to 6 days. Yield: 1⅓ cups.

PER TABLESPOON: 16 CALORIES (39% FROM FAT)
FAT 0.7G (SATURATED FAT 0.5G)
PROTEIN 1.8G   CARBOHYDRATE 0.5G
CHOLESTEROL 3MG   SODIUM 78MG

CURRIED PEPPERCORN MUSTARD

½ cup Dijon mustard
½ cup nonfat sour cream
1 tablespoon black peppercorns, crushed
1 teaspoon curry powder
½ teaspoon dried tarragon, crushed
¼ teaspoon ground allspice

Combine all ingredients in a small bowl; stir well. Cover and chill at least 8 hours. Serve as a sandwich spread or with chicken or pork. Yield: 1 cup.

PER TABLESPOON: 17 CALORIES (32% FROM FAT)
FAT 0.6G (SATURATED FAT 0.0G)
PROTEIN 0.6G   CARBOHYDRATE 1.7G
CHOLESTEROL 0MG   SODIUM 228MG

PEPPERED CHEESE CHIPS

12 (6-inch) flour tortillas
Vegetable cooking spray
¼ cup grated Parmesan cheese
½ teaspoon ground red pepper
½ teaspoon black pepper

Lightly coat tortillas with cooking spray; cut each tortilla into 4 wedges. Combine cheese and peppers; stir well, and sprinkle over tortilla wedges. Arrange wedges in a single layer on a baking sheet. Bake at 350° for 10 minutes or until crisp and lightly browned. Yield: 4 dozen.

PER CHIP: 31 CALORIES (23% FROM FAT)
FAT 0.8G (SATURATED FAT 0.2G)
PROTEIN 0.9G   CARBOHYDRATE 4.9G
CHOLESTEROL 0MG   SODIUM 50MG

ITALIAN SEASONED SNACK MIX

The egg whites help moisten the cereal mixture and create a crispy coating on the mixture as it cooks.

4 cups crispy corn-and-rice cereal
2 cups oyster crackers
2 cups small fat-free pretzels
¼ cup reduced-calorie stick margarine, melted
2 egg whites, lightly beaten
¼ cup grated Parmesan cheese
1 tablespoon dried Italian seasoning
Vegetable cooking spray

Combine first 3 ingredients in a large bowl. Combine margarine and egg whites in a small bowl; stir well with a wire whisk. Pour margarine mixture over cereal mixture; toss lightly to coat. Sprinkle with cheese and Italian seasoning; toss lightly.

Spread mixture in two 15- x 10- x 1-inch jellyroll pans coated with cooking spray. Bake at 300° for 25 minutes or until crisp, stirring occasionally. Cool completely. Store in an airtight container. Yield: 24 (¼-cup) servings.

PER SERVING: 62 CALORIES (29% FROM FAT)
FAT 2.0G (SATURATED FAT 0.3G)
PROTEIN 1.6G CARBOHYDRATE 9.9G
CHOLESTEROL 1MG SODIUM 188MG

APPLE BUTTER

(pictured on page 140)

You can use any good cooking apple in place of Winesap.

4 large Winesap apples, peeled, cored, and
     each cut into 8 wedges
1 cup unsweetened apple juice
½ cup firmly packed brown sugar
1 teaspoon ground cinnamon
¼ teaspoon salt
¼ teaspoon ground cloves
⅛ teaspoon ground allspice

Combine apple wedges and juice in a large saucepan; bring to a boil. Cover, reduce heat, and simmer 12 minutes or until apple is tender, stirring occasionally. Drain apple, discarding liquid.

Position knife blade in food processor bowl; add apple. Process 1 minute or until smooth. Return to saucepan; add brown sugar and remaining ingredients, stirring well.

Cook, uncovered, over medium heat 20 minutes or until mixture is very thick, stirring often. Spoon into hot sterilized jars, filling to ¼-inch from top; wipe jar rims. Cover at once with metal lids, and screw on bands. Store in refrigerator up to 3 weeks. Serve with pancakes, bagels, or low-fat biscuits. Yield: 2½ cups.

PER TABLESPOON: 25 CALORIES (4% FROM FAT)
FAT 0.1G (SATURATED FAT 0.0G)
PROTEIN 0.0G CARBOHYDRATE 6.4G
CHOLESTEROL 0MG SODIUM 16MG

CRANBERRY JEZEBEL SAUCE

(pictured on page 7)

1 cup water
½ cup sugar
½ cup firmly packed brown sugar
1 (12-ounce) bag fresh or frozen cranberries
3 tablespoons prepared horseradish
1 tablespoon Dijon mustard

Combine first 3 ingredients in a medium saucepan; stir well. Bring to a boil over medium heat; add cranberries. Return to a boil, and cook 10 minutes, stirring occasionally. Spoon into a bowl; cool to room temperature. Stir in horseradish and mustard; cover and chill. Serve with beef or pork; or pour over cream cheese, and serve with crackers. Store in an airtight container in refrigerator. Yield: 2½ cups.

PER TABLESPOON: 22 CALORIES (4% FROM FAT)
FAT 0.1G (SATURATED FAT 0.0G)
PROTEIN 0.1G CARBOHYDRATE 5.5G
CHOLESTEROL 0MG SODIUM 13MG

CRANBERRY CONSERVE

(pictured on page 2)

2 medium-size navel oranges
¾ cup sugar
1 cup water
3 cups fresh cranberries
¼ cup chopped walnuts

Grate 1 tablespoon rind from oranges; set aside. Peel and section oranges over a large bowl, reserving juice. Set orange sections and orange juice aside.

Combine sugar and water in a medium nonaluminum saucepan; bring to a boil over medium heat. Add cranberries; return to a boil, and cook 3 minutes or until cranberries pop, stirring occasionally. Add orange sections and juice; cook 10 minutes or until thickened, stirring often.

Remove from heat; stir in grated orange rind and walnuts. Cool to room temperature. Cover and chill. Serve with pork or poultry. Yield: 3½ cups.

PER TABLESPOON: 18 CALORIES (15% FROM FAT)
FAT 0.3G (SATURATED FAT 0.0G)
PROTEIN 0.2G   CARBOHYDRATE 4.0G
CHOLESTEROL 0MG   SODIUM 0MG

PEAR AND APPLE CHUTNEY

(pictured on page 2)

2½ cups peeled, coarsely chopped fresh pear
2½ cups peeled, coarsely chopped cooking
    apple
1 cup coarsely chopped onion
¾ cup firmly packed brown sugar
⅓ cup raisins
⅔ cup cider vinegar
½ cup water
2 teaspoons mustard seeds
2 teaspoons ground ginger
1 teaspoon ground allspice

Combine all ingredients in a large saucepan, stirring well; bring mixture to a boil. Reduce heat, and simmer, uncovered, 1 hour and 40 minutes or until mixture is thickened, stirring occasionally.

Remove chutney from heat, and cool to room temperature; cover and chill thoroughly. Serve with pork or poultry. Yield: 3 cups.

PER TABLESPOON: 29 CALORIES (3% FROM FAT)
FAT 0.1G (SATURATED FAT 0.0G)
PROTEIN 0.2G   CARBOHYDRATE 7.5G
CHOLESTEROL 0MG   SODIUM 2MG

CRANBERRY WINE VINEGAR

1 cup white vinegar
½ cup dry white wine
½ cup cranberry juice cocktail
2 cloves garlic, minced
Fresh rosemary sprigs (optional)

Combine first 4 ingredients in a pint-size jar; cover tightly, and shake vigorously. Chill at least 8 hours. Place rosemary sprigs in vinegar mixture, if desired. Use in salad dressings or vinaigrettes. Yield: 2 cups.

PER TABLESPOON: 6 CALORIES (0% FROM FAT)
FAT 0.0G (SATURATED FAT 0.0G)
PROTEIN 0.0G   CARBOHYDRATE 1.1G
CHOLESTEROL 0MG   SODIUM 0MG

Gift Giving

Imaginative packaging of food gifts doesn't have to be elaborate or expensive. For example, you can pour sauces or vinegars into a syrup pitcher, an interesting cruet, or an unusual shaped jar. Cover the container with holiday fabric, wax paper, or plastic wrap, and secure with ribbon or a strip of gold elastic. (See page 137 for more ideas.)

BANANA TREATS

1 cup sugar
½ cup stick margarine, softened
⅓ cup mashed ripe banana
1 teaspoon vanilla extract
1 egg
2¼ cups all-purpose flour
1 teaspoon baking soda
⅛ teaspoon ground nutmeg
1½ cups low-fat granola (without
　　raisins)
Vegetable cooking spray

Beat sugar and margarine at medium speed of an electric mixer until fluffy (about 3 minutes). Add banana, vanilla, and egg; beat well. Combine flour, baking soda, and nutmeg, stirring well; add to margarine mixture, beating well. Stir in granola.

Drop dough by level tablespoonfuls onto cookie sheets coated with cooking spray. Bake at 325° for 12 minutes or until lightly browned; cool on cookie sheets 1 minute. Remove from cookie sheets, and cool completely on wire racks. Yield: 3 dozen.

PER COOKIE: 92 CALORIES (29% FROM FAT)
FAT 3.0G (SATURATED FAT 0.6G)
PROTEIN 1.4G   CARBOHYDRATE 14.9G
CHOLESTEROL 6MG   SODIUM 71MG

CHEWY COCONUT COOKIES

2 cups all-purpose flour
¾ teaspoon baking soda
¼ teaspoon salt
⅔ cup sugar
⅓ cup dark corn syrup
3 tablespoons vegetable oil
1 teaspoon vanilla extract
1 teaspoon coconut extract
2 egg whites
⅓ cup flaked sweetened coconut
Vegetable cooking spray
2 tablespoons flaked sweetened coconut,
　　toasted

Combine first 4 ingredients in a large bowl, stirring well. Combine corn syrup and next 4 ingredients, stirring well; add to flour mixture, stirring just until dry ingredients are moistened. Stir in ⅓ cup coconut.

Drop dough by level tablespoonfuls onto cookie sheets coated with cooking spray. Sprinkle toasted coconut over cookies; bake at 350° for 8 minutes. Cool on cookie sheets 1 minute. Remove from cookie sheets; cool on wire racks. Yield: 3 dozen.

PER COOKIE: 66 CALORIES (22% FROM FAT)
FAT 1.6G (SATURATED FAT 0.6G)
PROTEIN 0.9G   CARBOHYDRATE 11.9G
CHOLESTEROL 0MG   SODIUM 52MG

DATE-SUGAR COOKIES

¾ cup sugar
¼ cup stick margarine, softened
1 teaspoon vanilla extract
1 egg
1¼ cups all-purpose flour
¼ cup yellow cornmeal
¾ teaspoon baking soda
⅓ cup finely chopped pecans, toasted
⅓ cup chopped pitted dates
Vegetable cooking spray

Beat sugar and margarine at medium speed of an electric mixer until fluffy (about 3 minutes). Add vanilla and egg; beat well. Combine flour, cornmeal, and baking soda, stirring well. Add to margarine mixture, beating well. Stir in pecans and dates.

Drop dough by level tablespoonfuls onto cookie sheets coated with cooking spray. Bake at 350° for 10 minutes; cool on cookie sheets 2 minutes. Remove from cookie sheets; cool on wire racks. Yield: 2½ dozen.

PER COOKIE: 72 CALORIES (34% FROM FAT)
FAT 2.7G (SATURATED FAT 0.4G)
PROTEIN 1.0G   CARBOHYDRATE 11.3G
CHOLESTEROL 7MG   SODIUM 41MG

From left: *Date-Sugar Cookies, Mint-Chocolate Drops (page 128), Frosted Orange Drops (page 128), and Chewy Coconut Cookies*

MINT-CHOCOLATE DROPS

(pictured on page 127)

⅔ cup sugar
⅓ cup molasses
2 tablespoons vegetable oil
1 egg
1 egg white
2 cups all-purpose flour
1 teaspoon baking soda
¼ teaspoon salt
½ cup unsweetened cocoa
⅔ cup mint-flavored semisweet chocolate
   morsels, divided
2 tablespoons fat-free milk
1¼ teaspoons vanilla extract
Vegetable cooking spray

Combine first 3 ingredients in a large bowl; beat at medium speed of an electric mixer until blended. Add egg and egg white; beat well. Combine flour and next 3 ingredients, stirring well; gradually add to molasses mixture, beating well. Stir in ½ cup chocolate morsels, milk, and vanilla.

Drop dough by level tablespoonfuls onto cookie sheets coated with cooking spray. Bake at 325° for 12 minutes; cool on cookie sheets 1 minute. Remove from cookie sheets; cool on wire racks.

Place remaining chocolate morsels in a small heavy-duty, zip-top plastic bag; seal bag. Submerge bag in very hot water until morsels melt. Snip a tiny hole in one corner of bag; drizzle chocolate over cookies. Yield: 3 dozen.

PER COOKIE: 79 CALORIES (23% FROM FAT)
FAT 2.0G (SATURATED FAT 0.3G)
PROTEIN 1.5G CARBOHYDRATE 13.6G
CHOLESTEROL 6MG SODIUM 57MG

FROSTED ORANGE DROPS

(pictured on page 127)

¾ cup sugar
⅓ cup stick margarine, softened
¼ cup orange juice concentrate, thawed and
   undiluted
1 egg
2 cups all-purpose flour
1 teaspoon baking soda
¼ teaspoon salt
2 teaspoons grated orange rind
Vegetable cooking spray
¾ cup sifted powdered sugar
1 tablespoon unsweetened orange juice

Beat sugar and margarine at medium speed of an electric mixer until light and fluffy (about 3 minutes). Add orange juice concentrate and egg; beat well. Combine flour and next 3 ingredients, stirring well; gradually add to margarine mixture, beating well.

Drop dough by level tablespoonfuls onto cookie sheets coated with cooking spray. Bake at 350° for 12 minutes or until lightly browned; cool on cookie sheets 1 minute. Remove from cookie sheets; cool completely on wire racks.

Combine powdered sugar and orange juice; stir well, and drizzle over cooled cookies. Yield: 2 dozen.

PER COOKIE: 108 CALORIES (24% FROM FAT)
FAT 2.9G (SATURATED FAT 0.6G)
PROTEIN 1.5G CARBOHYDRATE 19.3G
CHOLESTEROL 9MG SODIUM 110MG

Cookie Tips

• To get the number of cookies indicated on each recipe, drop the dough using the tablespoon attached to your set of measuring spoons.

• Use regular stick margarine instead of the reduced-fat version when baking cookies (unless indicated otherwise).

Oatmeal-Spice Cookies

OATMEAL-SPICE COOKIES

1½ cups all-purpose flour
1 teaspoon baking soda
½ teaspoon salt
1 teaspoon ground cinnamon
1 teaspoon ground nutmeg
½ teaspoon ground ginger
1 cup firmly packed brown sugar
½ cup sugar
½ cup stick margarine, softened
3 tablespoons light-colored corn syrup
1½ teaspoons vanilla extract
2 egg whites
1 egg
3 cups quick-cooking oats
1⅓ cups raisins
Vegetable cooking spray

Combine first 6 ingredients; set aside. Combine brown sugar and next 6 ingredients in a large bowl; beat at medium speed of an electric mixer until well blended. Stir in oats and raisins; let stand 5 minutes. Stir in flour mixture.

Drop dough by level tablespoonfuls, 2 inches apart, onto cookie sheets coated with cooking spray. Bake at 350° for 10 minutes or until lightly browned. Remove cookies from cookie sheets; cool on wire racks. Yield: 4½ dozen.

Note: Store cookies in an airtight container up to 1 week.

PER COOKIE: 79 CALORIES (24% FROM FAT)
FAT 2.1G (SATURATED FAT 0.4G)
PROTEIN 1.5G   CARBOHYDRATE 13.9G
CHOLESTEROL 4MG   SODIUM 71MG

POPPY SEED-ALMOND COOKIES

1 cup sugar
⅓ cup stick margarine, softened
2 tablespoons light-colored corn syrup
1½ teaspoons almond extract
1 egg
1 egg white
2¼ cups all-purpose flour
2 tablespoons poppy seeds
1 teaspoon baking soda
Vegetable cooking spray

Beat sugar and margarine at medium speed of an electric mixer until fluffy (about 3 minutes). Add corn syrup and next 3 ingredients; beat well. Combine flour, poppy seeds, and baking soda, stirring well; add to margarine mixture, beating well.

Drop dough by rounded tablespoonfuls onto cookie sheets coated with cooking spray. Bake at 350° for 10 minutes or until lightly browned; cool on cookie sheets 1 minute. Remove from cookie sheets; cool on wire racks. Yield: 3 dozen.

PER COOKIE: 74 CALORIES (26% FROM FAT)
FAT 2.1G (SATURATED FAT 0.4G)
PROTEIN 1.2G   CARBOHYDRATE 12.5G
CHOLESTEROL 6MG   SODIUM 59MG

Chocolate Icebox Cookies and Vanilla Icebox Cookies (page 132)

CHOCOLATE ICEBOX COOKIES

Rolling dough in turbinado sugar gives cookies a sugary edge. Turbinado sugar is a coarse, blond-colored sugar with a delicate molasses flavor; look for it in the supermarket's baking section.

¼ cup stick margarine, softened
⅔ cup sugar
1 teaspoon vanilla extract
1 egg white
¾ cup all-purpose flour
¼ teaspoon baking soda
⅛ teaspoon salt
¼ cup unsweetened cocoa
2 tablespoons turbinado sugar
Vegetable cooking spray

Beat softened margarine at medium speed of an electric mixer until light and fluffy. Gradually add ⅔ cup sugar, beating until well blended. Add vanilla and egg white, beating well. Combine flour and next 3 ingredients, stirring mixture well; add to margarine mixture, stirring until well blended.

Turn dough out onto wax paper; shape into a 6-inch log. Wrap log in wax paper; freeze 3 hours or until very firm.

Roll log in turbinado sugar. Cut log into 24 (¼-inch) slices; place slices, 1 inch apart, on cookie sheets coated with cooking spray. Bake at 350° for 8 to 10 minutes. Remove from cookie sheets; cool on wire racks. Yield: 2 dozen.

Note: For Chocolate-Peppermint Icebox Cookies, substitute 1 teaspoon peppermint extract for vanilla.

PER COOKIE: 61 CALORIES (31% FROM FAT)
FAT 2.1G (SATURATED FAT 0.5G)
PROTEIN 0.8G CARBOHYDRATE 9.8G
CHOLESTEROL 0MG SODIUM 51MG

PEANUT BUTTER ICEBOX COOKIES

For variety, add 1 ounce grated semisweet chocolate to flour mixture.

3 tablespoons stick margarine, softened
2 tablespoons chunky peanut butter
½ cup firmly packed brown sugar
¼ cup sugar
1 teaspoon vanilla extract
1 egg white
1 cup all-purpose flour
¼ teaspoon baking soda
⅛ teaspoon salt
Vegetable cooking spray

Beat margarine and peanut butter at medium speed of an electric mixer until light and fluffy. Gradually add sugars, beating until well blended. Add vanilla and egg white, beating well. Combine flour, soda, and salt; add to margarine mixture, stirring well.

Turn dough out onto wax paper, and shape into a 6-inch log. Wrap log in wax paper; freeze 3 hours.

Cut log into 24 (¼-inch) slices; place slices, 1 inch apart, on cookie sheets coated with cooking spray. Bake at 350° for 8 to 10 minutes. Remove from cookie sheets; cool on wire racks. Yield: *2 dozen.*

PER COOKIE: 69 CALORIES (31% FROM FAT)
FAT 2.4G (SATURATED FAT 0.4G)
PROTEIN 1.2G   CARBOHYDRATE 10.8G
CHOLESTEROL 9MG   SODIUM 53MG

Cookie Pinwheels

Roll Peanut Butter Icebox Cookie and Chocolate Icebox Cookie doughs separately between two sheets of wax paper to form two 12-inch squares. Freeze 15 minutes.

Remove wax paper; stack dough portions, one on top of the other. Roll together into a log; wrap in wax paper. Freeze 3 hours.

Cut log into ¼-inch slices with dental floss. Place slices on a cookie sheet, and bake at 350° for 10 minutes.

VANILLA ICEBOX COOKIES

(pictured on page 130)

¼ cup stick margarine, softened
⅔ cup sugar
1 teaspoon vanilla extract
1 egg white
1 cup all-purpose flour
¼ teaspoon baking soda
⅛ teaspoon salt
Vegetable cooking spray

Beat margarine at medium speed of an electric mixer until light and fluffy. Gradually add sugar, beating at medium speed until well blended. Add vanilla and egg white, beating well. Combine flour, soda, and salt, stirring well; add to margarine mixture, stirring until well blended. Turn dough out onto wax paper; shape into a 6-inch log. Wrap log in wax paper; freeze 3 hours or until very firm.

Cut into 24 (¼-inch) slices; place slices, 1 inch apart, on cookie sheets coated with cooking spray. Bake at 350° for 8 to 10 minutes. Remove from cookie sheets; cool on wire racks. Yield: 2 dozen.

PER COOKIE: 59 CALORIES (31% FROM FAT)
FAT 2.0G (SATURATED FAT 0.4G)
PROTEIN 0.7G CARBOHYDRATE 9.6G
CHOLESTEROL 0MG SODIUM 50MG

Steps to Success

• Too much flour will make icebox cookies dry and crumbly. To measure flour accurately, lightly spoon it into a dry measuring cup, leveling it with the flat side of a knife.

• If the dough is too soft to shape, simply chill until slightly firm.

• Each time you slice off a cookie from the log, turn log one quarter to keep it from becoming flat on one side.

• You can freeze logs up to one month, but be sure to double-wrap them for extra protection.

FROSTED SUGAR COOKIES

(pictured on cover)

¾ cup plus 2 tablespoons firmly packed brown sugar
½ cup stick margarine, softened
2 tablespoons fat-free milk
2 teaspoons vanilla extract
1 egg
3 cups all-purpose flour
1½ teaspoons baking powder
½ teaspoon salt
2 teaspoons all-purpose flour, divided
Vegetable cooking spray
1½ cups sifted powdered sugar
3¾ teaspoons water

Beat brown sugar and margarine at medium speed of an electric mixer until light and fluffy. Add milk, vanilla, and egg, beating well. Combine 3 cups flour, baking powder, and salt, stirring well; gradually add to margarine mixture, beating well. Cover and chill at least 2 hours.

Divide dough in half. Work with 1 portion at a time, storing remainder in refrigerator. Sprinkle 1 teaspoon flour evenly over work surface. Turn dough out onto floured surface; roll to ⅛-inch thickness. Cut into rounds with a 2-inch cookie cutter, or cut into decorative shapes; place rounds, 2 inches apart, on cookie sheets coated with cooking spray.

Bake at 350° for 6 to 8 minutes or until edges of cookies are lightly browned. Remove from cookie sheets; cool on wire racks. Repeat procedure with remaining 1 teaspoon flour and remaining dough.

Combine powdered sugar and water. Pipe or spread frosting on cookies. Yield: 6 dozen.

PER COOKIE: 52 CALORIES (24% FROM FAT)
FAT 1.4G (SATURATED FAT 0.3G)
PROTEIN 0.7G CARBOHYDRATE 9.2G
CHOLESTEROL 3MG SODIUM 42MG

MINT-CHOCOLATE TRUFFLES

⅓ cup mint-flavored semisweet chocolate
    morsels
4 ounces block-style ⅓-less-fat cream cheese,
    softened
1 (16-ounce) package powdered sugar, sifted
½ cup unsweetened cocoa
¼ cup mint-flavored semisweet chocolate
    morsels

Place ⅓ cup chocolate morsels in a glass bowl, and microwave at HIGH 1 minute or until almost melted, stirring until smooth; cool.

Add cream cheese to melted chocolate, beating at medium speed of an electric mixer until smooth; add powdered sugar, beating until well blended. Press mixture into a 6-inch square on plastic wrap; cover with additional plastic wrap. Chill at least 1 hour.

Remove top sheet of plastic wrap; slice mixture into 48 squares. Roll each square into a ball; place on wax paper. Roll truffles in cocoa.

Place ¼ cup chocolate morsels in a heavy-duty, zip-top plastic bag; microwave at HIGH 1 minute or until soft. Knead bag until smooth. Snip a tiny hole in one corner of bag; drizzle chocolate over balls rolled in cocoa. Serve at room temperature. Yield: 4 dozen.

Note: For a variation, roll truffles in ½ cup sifted powdered sugar, omitting cocoa and ¼ cup chocolate morsels.

PER TRUFFLE: 57 CALORIES (21% FROM FAT)
FAT 1.3G (SATURATED FAT 0.8G)
PROTEIN 0.6G   CARBOHYDRATE 11.1G
CHOLESTEROL 2MG   SODIUM 10MG

Mint-Chocolate Truffles

Hazelnut Biscotti

HAZELNUT BISCOTTI

¾ cup hazelnuts
3¾ cups plus 2 tablespoons all-purpose flour
1½ teaspoons baking powder
⅛ teaspoon salt
1½ cups sugar
¼ teaspoon ground nutmeg
⅓ cup Frangelico or other hazelnut-flavored liqueur
¼ cup plus 1 tablespoon stick margarine, melted
2 teaspoons vanilla extract
2 eggs
2 egg whites
Vegetable cooking spray
1 egg white, lightly beaten

Place hazelnuts on a baking sheet. Bake at 350° for 15 minutes. Turn hazelnuts out onto a towel; let stand 1 minute. Roll up towel; rub nuts to remove skins. Set nuts aside.

Combine flour and next 4 ingredients in a large bowl; add hazelnuts. Combine Frangelico and next 4 ingredients; add to flour mixture, stirring until well blended.

Turn dough out onto a lightly floured surface; knead 7 or 8 times. Divide dough into 6 equal portions. Shape each portion into a 10-inch-long roll. Place rolls on cookie sheets coated with cooking spray; flatten each roll to ¾-inch thickness. Brush rolls with lightly beaten egg white.

Bake at 350° for 20 minutes. Remove from cookie sheets; cool on wire racks. Slice each roll diagonally into 18 (½-inch) slices. Place slices, cut sides down, on cookie sheets. Bake at 350° for 20 minutes or until dry. Cool on wire racks. Yield: 9 dozen.

PER COOKIE: 42 CALORIES (28% FROM FAT)
FAT 1.3G (SATURATED FAT 0.2G)
PROTEIN 0.8G   CARBOHYDRATE 6.8G
CHOLESTEROL 4MG   SODIUM 16MG

BIZCOCHITOS

Anise seeds lend these cookies a mild licorice flavor.

¼ cup plus 1 tablespoon stick margarine, softened
¾ cup plus 2 teaspoons sugar, divided
1 egg
1 teaspoon vanilla extract
1¾ cups sifted cake flour
2 teaspoons anise seeds
1 teaspoon baking powder
⅛ teaspoon salt
½ teaspoon ground cinnamon

Beat margarine at medium speed of an electric mixer until creamy; gradually add ¾ cup sugar, beating until mixture is light and fluffy. Add egg and vanilla, beating well. Combine flour and next 3 ingredients, stirring well; add to margarine mixture, stirring until well blended. Shape dough into a ball; wrap in heavy-duty plastic wrap. Freeze dough 40 minutes.

Remove plastic wrap; roll dough to a 1/16-inch thickness on a lightly floured surface. Cut into rounds with a 2-inch round cutter; place rounds on cookie sheets. Combine remaining 2 teaspoons sugar and cinnamon; sprinkle over cookies. Bake at 350° for 10 minutes. Remove from cookie sheets; cool on wire racks. Store in an airtight container. Yield: 4 dozen.

PER COOKIE: 40 CALORIES (29% FROM FAT)
FAT 1.3G (SATURATED FAT 0.3G)
PROTEIN 0.5G   CARBOHYDRATE 6.5G
CHOLESTEROL 5MG   SODIUM 28MG

SPICED HEART COOKIES

¼ cup plus 2 tablespoons reduced-calorie stick margarine, softened
⅔ cup sugar
¼ cup molasses
1 egg white
2⅓ cups all-purpose flour
1½ teaspoons baking soda
¼ teaspoon salt
1¾ teaspoons ground cinnamon
¾ teaspoon pumpkin pie spice
Vegetable cooking spray
1 tablespoon sugar

Beat margarine at medium speed of an electric mixer until creamy; gradually add ⅔ cup sugar, beating well. Add molasses and egg white, beating well. Combine flour and next 4 ingredients, stirring well; gradually add to margarine mixture, beating well. Shape dough into a ball; cover and chill at least 1 hour.

Divide dough into 2 portions. Roll 1 portion between two sheets of heavy-duty plastic wrap to ¼-inch thickness. Remove top sheet of plastic wrap; cut with a 2-inch heart-shaped cookie cutter. Place cookies on a cookie sheet coated with cooking spray. Repeat procedure with remaining dough. Sprinkle cookies evenly with 1 tablespoon sugar. Bake at 350° for 10 to 12 minutes or until golden. Remove from cookie sheets; cool on wire racks. Yield: 28 cookies.

PER COOKIE: 80 CALORIES (19% FROM FAT)
FAT 1.7G (SATURATED FAT 0.2G)
PROTEIN 1.2G CARBOHYDRATE 15.3G
CHOLESTEROL 0MG SODIUM 115MG

LINZER COOKIES

(pictured on cover)

Reminiscent of old-fashioned English jam tarts, these scalloped sandwich cookies are filled with raspberry jam and dusted with powdered sugar.

¼ cup plus 1 tablespoon stick margarine, softened
½ cup sugar
1 teaspoon vanilla extract
2 egg whites
1½ cups plus 2 tablespoons all-purpose flour
½ cup cornstarch
⅓ cup ground blanched almonds (about 1 ounce)
1 teaspoon baking powder
Vegetable cooking spray
¼ cup plus 2 teaspoons seedless red raspberry jam
2 tablespoons powdered sugar

Beat margarine at medium speed of an electric mixer; add ½ cup sugar, beating until blended. Add vanilla and egg whites, beating well. Combine flour and next 3 ingredients; add to margarine mixture, beating well.

Divide dough into 4 equal portions. Working with 1 portion of dough at a time, roll dough to ⅛-inch thickness on a lightly floured surface.

Cut dough, using a 2¼-inch scalloped cookie cutter. Place cookies, 1 inch apart, on cookie sheets coated with cooking spray. Cut centers from half of cookies with a ¾-inch round canapé cutter. Bake at 350° for 8 minutes. (Do not let cookies brown.) Remove from cookie sheets; cool on wire racks. Repeat procedure with remaining dough.

Spread ½ teaspoon jam on flat side of each solid cookie; top with cutout cookies. Sift powdered sugar over cookies. Store in an airtight container. Yield: 28 cookies.

Note: Cookies will soften when stored overnight in an airtight container.

PER COOKIE: 86 CALORIES (28% FROM FAT)
FAT 2.7G (SATURATED FAT 0.5G)
PROTEIN 1.3G CARBOHYDRATE 14.2G
CHOLESTEROL 0MG SODIUM 40MG

JOULUTORTUT

*These prune-filled pinwheel cookies have
their origin in Finland.*

½ cup sugar
¼ cup stick margarine, softened
½ teaspoon grated orange rind
1 egg, lightly beaten
2 cups all-purpose flour
¼ teaspoon baking soda
¼ teaspoon salt
2 tablespoons ice water
½ cup pitted prunes, chopped
3 tablespoons water
⅛ teaspoon ground cinnamon
½ teaspoon vanilla extract
Vegetable cooking spray
2 teaspoons powdered sugar

Beat sugar and margarine at medium speed of an
electric mixer until light and fluffy (about 5 minutes). Add orange rind and egg; beat 2 minutes or
until well blended. Combine flour, soda, and salt;
gradually add to margarine mixture, beating at low
speed until mixture resembles coarse meal.
Sprinkle ice water, 1 tablespoon at a time, over surface; toss with a fork until dry ingredients are
moistened. Gently press mixture into a ball; wrap
in heavy-duty plastic wrap, and freeze 30 minutes.

Combine prunes, 3 tablespoons water, and
cinnamon in a small saucepan. Cook over medium-
low heat 5 minutes or until prunes are softened.
Remove from heat; stir in vanilla. Position knife
blade in food processor bowl; add prune mixture.
Process until smooth; set aside.

Divide dough in half. Work with 1 portion at a
time, storing remainder in refrigerator. Turn dough
out onto a lightly floured surface; knead 8 or 9
times. Roll dough to ⅛-inch thickness. Cut dough
into 20 (2¼-inch) squares; carefully place squares
on cookie sheets coated with cooking spray.
Partially cut squares diagonally from corners in
toward center.

Spoon ¼ teaspoon prune mixture into center of
each square. Using tip of a knife, lift up and fold
every other point over prune mixture, forming a
pinwheel. Gently pinch points to seal.

Joulutortut

Bake at 375° for 9 minutes or until lightly
browned. Cool on wire racks. Sprinkle with powdered sugar. Repeat procedure with remaining
dough and prune mixture. Yield: 40 cookies.

PER COOKIE: 49 CALORIES (26% FROM FAT)
FAT 1.4G (SATURATED FAT 0.3G)
PROTEIN 0.9G   CARBOHYDRATE 8.3G
CHOLESTEROL 6MG   SODIUM 38MG

Festive Gifts

Here are some innovative ways to dress up
cookies for gift giving.
• Before the holidays arrive, look for unique
wrapping papers, tins, and ribbon in craft stores.
• Pack cookies in colorful miniature paper
bags or in wine bags that you've cut to suit
the size you need; tie with ribbon.
• Place small treats, such as Mint-Chocolate
Truffles (page 133), in miniature baking cups.
Then nestle them in a long, thin box and tie
with French wire ribbon.

SPRINGERLE

This anise-flavored cookie originated centuries ago in Germany and is still one of its most famous Christmas treats.

4 eggs
1¾ cups sugar
1 teaspoon grated lemon rind
1 teaspoon anise extract
4¼ cups all-purpose flour, divided
1 teaspoon baking powder
½ teaspoon salt
Vegetable cooking spray

Beat eggs in a large bowl at medium speed of a heavy-duty stand-up mixer 1 minute. Gradually add sugar, beating at high speed 10 minutes. Add lemon rind and anise extract; beat well. Combine 4 cups flour, baking powder, and salt; gradually add to egg mixture, beating at low speed until well blended.

Divide dough in half, and shape each portion into a ball. Wrap each portion in plastic wrap; chill dough and a cookie mold with 2- x 1½-inch imprints 1 hour.

Place 1 portion of dough on a well-floured surface; sprinkle dough with flour. Roll to ¼-inch thickness, and add enough of remaining flour to keep dough from sticking to surface and rolling pin. Coat cookie mold with cooking spray, and press mold firmly into dough. Remove mold; let dough stand 5 minutes. Cut cookies apart; place on cookie sheets covered with parchment paper or unglazed brown paper (do not use recycled paper). Cover with a towel, and let stand at room temperature 24 hours to dry. Repeat procedure with remaining dough and flour.

Bake at 275° for 15 minutes or until firm when lightly touched. Cool on wire racks. Store loosely covered. Yield: 9 dozen.

PER COOKIE: 32 CALORIES (6% FROM FAT)
FAT 0.2G (SATURATED FAT 0.1G)
PROTEIN 0.7G CARBOHYDRATE 6.8G
CHOLESTEROL 8MG SODIUM 16MG

FRANKFURTER BRENTEN

(pictured on page 120)

These dainty marzipan cookies derive their name from Frankfurt, Germany, where they were first introduced.

1¾ cups sifted powdered sugar
1 cup almond paste
½ cup plus 3 tablespoons all-purpose flour, divided
3 teaspoons rose water or water
1 egg white

Combine powdered sugar, almond paste, ⅓ cup plus 2 tablespoons flour, rose water, and egg white in a large bowl. Knead gently until dry ingredients are moistened.

Turn dough out onto a lightly floured surface. Knead until smooth (about 6 minutes); add enough of remaining flour, 2 teaspoons at a time, to keep dough from sticking to hands. Roll dough to ⅛-inch thickness on a lightly floured surface.

Using a petite cookie mold with 1¼-inch-square imprints, press mold firmly into dough to imprint. Remove mold; cut cookie squares apart, and place on baking sheets covered with parchment paper or unglazed brown paper (do not use recycled paper). Cover with a towel, and let stand at room temperature in a cool, dry place for 24 hours to dry.

Bake cookies at 275° for 12 minutes. Cool on wire racks. Yield: 7½ dozen.

PER COOKIE: 24 CALORIES (26% FROM FAT)
FAT 0.7G (SATURATED FAT 0.1G)
PROTEIN 0.4G CARBOHYDRATE 4.2G
CHOLESTEROL 0MG SODIUM 1MG

Almond Chess Bars

ALMOND CHESS BARS

2½ cups sifted powdered sugar
½ cup reduced-calorie stick margarine, melted
1 tablespoon water
1½ teaspoons almond extract
1 teaspoon imitation butter flavoring
3 egg whites
1 egg
1 (18.25-ounce) package light yellow cake mix
1 (8-ounce) tub nonfat cream cheese, softened
Vegetable cooking spray
2 teaspoons powdered sugar

Combine first 9 ingredients in a large mixing bowl; beat at medium speed of an electric mixer until smooth. Pour batter into a 13- x 9- x 2-inch baking pan coated with cooking spray. Bake at 350° for 45 minutes or until golden. Cool completely in pan on a wire rack. Sprinkle with 2 teaspoons powdered sugar. Cut into bars. Yield: 3 dozen.

PER BAR: 117 CALORIES (19% FROM FAT)
FAT 2.5G (SATURATED FAT 0.6G)
PROTEIN 2.3G CARBOHYDRATE 20.2G
CHOLESTEROL 7MG SODIUM 205MG

FUDGY CHOCOLATE BROWNIES

¼ cup plus 1 tablespoon stick margarine
1 (1-ounce) square unsweetened chocolate
⅔ cup Dutch process or unsweetened cocoa
1½ cups sugar
3 egg whites, lightly beaten
1 egg, lightly beaten
1 cup all-purpose flour
½ teaspoon baking powder
Vegetable cooking spray

Melt margarine and chocolate in a large saucepan over medium heat. Stir in cocoa; cook 1 minute. Stir in sugar, and cook 1 minute (mixture will almost form a ball and will be difficult to stir). Remove pan from heat; cool slightly. Gradually add warm chocolate mixture to egg whites and egg, stirring with a wire whisk until well blended. Combine flour and baking powder; add to chocolate mixture, stirring well.

Spoon batter into a 9-inch square baking pan coated with cooking spray. Bake at 325° for 30 minutes (do not overbake). Cool on a wire rack. Cut into bars. Yield: 20 bars.

PER BAR: 132 CALORIES (29% FROM FAT)
FAT 4.3G (SATURATED FAT 1.3G)
PROTEIN 2.5G CARBOHYDRATE 21.7G
CHOLESTEROL 11MG SODIUM 56MG

Fudgy Chocolate Brownies

Apple Butter (page 124) and Apple Spice Minicakes

APPLE SPICE MINICAKES

½ cup firmly packed brown sugar
¼ cup reduced-calorie stick margarine, softened
1 teaspoon vanilla extract
2 egg whites
2 cups all-purpose flour
2 teaspoons baking powder
½ teaspoon baking soda
¼ teaspoon salt
2 teaspoons ground cinnamon
¼ teaspoon ground nutmeg
⅔ cup nonfat buttermilk
1 cup finely chopped, unpeeled cooking apple
⅓ cup golden raisins
Vegetable cooking spray

Beat sugar and margarine at medium speed of an electric mixer until light and fluffy (about 5 minutes). Add vanilla and egg whites; beat at medium speed until well blended.

Combine flour and next 5 ingredients. With mixer running at low speed, add to margarine mixture alternately with buttermilk, beginning and ending with flour mixture. Stir in apple and raisins. Spoon batter evenly into two 5¾-x 3¼- x 2-inch aluminum foil loafpans coated with cooking spray.

Bake at 350° for 50 minutes or until a wooden pick inserted in center comes out clean. Cool on a wire rack. Yield: 2 loaves, 6 slices each.

PER SLICE: 160 CALORIES (16% FROM FAT)
FAT 2.8G (SATURATED FAT 0.1G)
PROTEIN 3.4G CARBOHYDRATE 31.2G
CHOLESTEROL 0MG SODIUM 233MG

INDEX

Almonds
  Bars, Almond Chess, 139
  Chips, Fluffy Fruit Dip with Almond, 31
  Cookies, Poppy Seed-Almond, 129
  Crème Caramel, Almond, 112
Appetizers
  Biscuits with Smoked Turkey, Cranberry, 30
  Bruschetta, White Bean, 49
  Chicken Bites with Cucumber Dip, Spicy, 46
  Chicken Drummettes with Pineapple Sauce,
    Teriyaki, 47
  Chicken Quesadillas, Santa Fe, 47
  Chips, Peppered Cheese, 123
  Dips
      Artichoke Dip, Hot, 42
      Blue Cheese Dip, Buffalo Shrimp with, 29
      Cucumber Dip, 47
      Deviled Dip, 29
      Fruit Dip with Almond Chips, Fluffy, 31
      Hummus with Pita Wedges, Red Bean, 42
      Pepper Dip, Roasted, 42
      Spinach-Ham Dip, 43
      Sweet Potato Dip, Roasted, 43
  Mix, Italian Seasoned Snack, 124
  Pâté, Smoked Turkey and Sun-Dried Tomato, 45
  Pizza, Artichoke and Red Pepper, 49
  Sauce, Pineapple, 47
  Shrimp with Blue Cheese Dip, Buffalo, 29
  Shrimp with Silken Tomato Vinaigrette, 48
  Spread, Shrimp-Chutney, 44
  Tarts, Crab-Artichoke, 48
  Turnovers, Curried Mushroom, 30
Apples
  Bread, Rum-Apple, 59
  Butter, Apple, 124
  Cake, Cinnamon-Apple, 102
  Chutney, Pear and Apple, 125
  Cider, Spiked Cranberry-Apple, 39
  Minicakes, Apple Spice, 140
  Rolls, Apple-Filled Sweet, 67
Applesauce, Homemade, 16
Applesauce Salad, Layered Cranberry-, 86
Apricot-Ginger Carrots, 90
Apricot-Prune Stuffing, Roast Pork with, 73
Artichokes
  Dip, Hot Artichoke, 42
  Pizza, Artichoke and Red Pepper, 49
  Tarts, Crab-Artichoke, 48

Banana Bread, Mom's, 59
Banana Treats, 126
Barley, Wild Rice, and Currant Pilaf, 13
Bean Bruschetta, White, 49
Bean Hummus with Pita Wedges, Red, 42
Beef
  Brisket with Vegetables, 71
  Filet Mignon with Mushroom-Wine Sauce, 70
  Roast, Fruited Cider, 72
  Roasting Tips, 72
Beverages
  Alcoholic
      Cider, Spiked Cranberry-Apple, 39
      Cocoa, Amaretto, 23
      Coffee, Irish, 20
      Coffee Royale, 40

  Cranberry Blush, Sparkling, 41
  Glögg, Holiday, 27
  Margaritas, Orange-Lime, 41
  Punch, Coffee-Kahlúa, 40
  Spritzers, Cranberry-Raspberry, 26
  Wine, Hot Mulled, 39
  Citrus Spritzer, 41
  Coffee Royale, 40
  Fruit Drink, Mulled, 38
  Garnishing beverages, 38
  Orange Twist, 39
  Punch, Cinnamon Candy, 40
  Scarlet Sipper, 33
  Tea, Spiced Fruit, 38
Biscotti, Hazelnut, 135
Biscuits
  Cheddar-Black Pepper Biscuits, 52
  Cranberry Biscuits with Smoked Turkey, 30
  Cranberry Silver Dollar Biscuits, 53
Bizcochitos, 135
Breads. *See also* specific types.
  Banana Bread, Mom's, 59
  Doughnuts, Spiced Baked, 54
  Dressing, Fruit and Cheese Bread, 95
  Gift of Bread, Give a, 59
  Grapefruit-Pecan Bread, 60
  Pear and Poppy Seed Loaf, 60
  Popovers, Easy, 54
  Popovers, Orange, 54
  Popovers, Savory Dillweed, 54
  Rum-Apple Bread, 59
  Scones, Cranberry, 23
  Scones, Date and Maple, 53
  Starter Food, 64
  Stuffing, New England Bread, 95
  Yeast
      Babka, Mocha, 63
      Cinnamon-Raisin Bread, 66
      Oat Bread with Prune Filling, Maple-, 62
      Saffron Bread, St. Lucia, 66
      Sourdough Bread, 64
      Sourdough Starter, 64
      Stollen, Dresdner, 65
Broccoli, Sesame, 89
Broccoli with Roasted Peppers, 13
Bruschetta, White Bean, 49
Butter, Apple, 124

Cakes
  Bundt Cake, Pumpkin-Spice, 104
  Bundt Cake, Zucchini-Streusel, 105
  Carrot Cake with Cream Cheese Frosting, 100
  Cheesecake, Chocolate Silk, 102
  Cheesecake, Maple-Pecan, 34
  Cinnamon-Apple Cake, 102
  Coffee Cake, Cardamom, 58
  Coffee Cake, Cinnamon-Streusel, 26
  Holiday Cake with Dried Fruit, 107
  Minicakes, Apple Spice, 140
  Pound Cake, Sour Cream, 107
  Soufflé Cake, Dark Chocolate, 100
  Upside-Down Cake, Cranberry, 104
Caramel, Almond Crème, 112
Caramel-Kahlúa Squares, 117
Carrot Cake with Cream Cheese Frosting, 100

Carrots, Apricot-Ginger, 90
Cheese
  Biscuits, Cheddar-Black Pepper, 52
  Bread Dressing, Fruit and Cheese, 95
  Cheesecake, Chocolate Silk, 102
  Cheesecake, Maple-Pecan, 34
  Chicken Rolls, Italian, 77
  Chips, Peppered Cheese, 123
  Dip, Buffalo Shrimp with Blue Cheese, 29
  Dip, Deviled, 29
  Frosting, Cream Cheese, 100
  Potted Herbed Cheese, 123
  Quiche, Ham and Cheese, 25
  Tart, Cream Cheese-Cranberry, 110
  Tiramisù, 115
Chicken
  Bites with Cucumber Dip, Spicy Chicken, 46
  Drummettes with Pineapple Sauce, Teriyaki
    Chicken, 47
  Quesadillas, Santa Fe Chicken, 47
  Roast Chicken, Grandma's Simple, 16
  Rolls, Italian Chicken, 77
Chips, Peppered Cheese, 123
Chocolate
  Brownie Dessert, Fudgy Mint, 115
  Brownies, Fudgy Chocolate, 139
  Cake, Dark Chocolate Soufflé, 100
  Cheesecake, Chocolate Silk, 102
  Cocoa, Amaretto, 23
  Cookies
      Icebox Cookies, Chocolate, 130
      Mint-Chocolate Drops, 128
      Pinwheels, Cookie, 131
  Mocha Babka, 63
  Pudding, Bittersweet Chocolate, 112
  Pudding, Black Bottom Cranberry, 113
  Soufflés, French Silk, 14
  Streusel, Chocolate, 63
  Tart, Double-Chocolate Cream, 108
  Truffles, Mint-Chocolate, 133
Chutney, Pear and Apple, 125
Chutney Spread, Shrimp-, 44
Cinnamon
  Bread, Cinnamon-Raisin, 66
  Cake, Cinnamon-Apple, 102
  Coffee Cake, Cinnamon-Streusel, 26
  Punch, Cinnamon Candy, 40
  Tart, Cinnamon-Pear, 20
Coconut
  Cookies, Chewy Coconut, 126
  Macaroon Tartlets, Lemon-, 31
  Macaroon Tart Shells, 31
Coffee
  Cake, Dark Chocolate Soufflé, 100
  Dessert, Coffee-Toffee, 118
  Irish Coffee, 20
  Mocha Babka, 63
  Punch, Coffee-Kahlúa, 40
  Royale, Coffee, 40
  Tiramisù, 115
Compote, Citrus and Dried Fruit, 116
Compote, Easy Fruit, 23
Cookies
  Bars, Almond Chess, 139
  Biscotti, Hazelnut, 135
  Brownies, Fudgy Chocolate, 139

Cookies *(continued)*

Drop
  Banana Treats, 126
  Coconut Cookies, Chewy, 126
  Date-Sugar Cookies, 126
  Mint-Chocolate Drops, 128
  Oatmeal-Spice Cookies, 129
  Orange Drops, Frosted, 128
  Poppy Seed-Almond Cookies, 129
Frankfurter Brenten, 138
Gifts, Festive, 137
Linzer Cookies, 136
Mandelbrot, 17
Refrigerator
  Bizcochitos, 135
  Chocolate Icebox Cookies, 130
  Joulutortut, 137
  Peanut Butter Icebox Cookies, 131
  Pinwheels, Cookie, 131
  Spiced Heart Cookies, 136
  Springerle, 138
  Sugar Cookies, Frosted, 132
  Vanilla Icebox Cookies, 132
Tips, Cookie, 128
Cornbread, Basic, 97
Cornbread Dressing, 96
Cornish Hens, Grecian, 77
Crab-Artichoke Tarts, 48
Crab Quiche Florentine, 25
Cranberries
  Biscuits, Cranberry Silver Dollar, 53
  Biscuits with Smoked Turkey, Cranberry, 30
  Blush, Sparkling Cranberry, 41
  Cake, Cranberry Upside-Down, 104
  Cider, Spiked Cranberry-Apple, 39
  Conserve, Cranberry, 125
  Ice, Cranberry, 118
  Muffins, Cranberry-Citrus, 56
  Pudding, Black Bottom Cranberry, 113
  Salad, Layered Cranberry-Applesauce, 86
  Sauce, Cranberry Jezebel, 124
  Scones, Cranberry, 23
  Sipper, Scarlet, 33
  Spritzers, Cranberry-Raspberry, 26
  Sweet Potatoes, Cranberry-Glazed, 14
  Tart, Cream Cheese-Cranberry, 110
  Vinegar, Cranberry Wine, 125
Crawfish, Fettuccine, 81
Creole, Spicy Shrimp, 82
Cucumber Dip, 47
Currant Pilaf, Barley, Wild Rice, and, 13
Curry
  Mustard, Curried Peppercorn, 123
  Turkey Ballottine, Curried, 78
  Turnovers, Curried Mushroom, 30

Date and Maple Scones, 53
Date-Sugar Cookies, 126
Degrease Turkey Drippings, How to, 97
Desserts. *See also* specific types.
  Brownie Dessert, Fudgy Mint, 115
  Compote, Citrus and Dried Fruit, 116
  Crème Caramel, Almond, 112
  Freezing desserts, 113
  Frozen
    Caramel-Kahlúa Squares, 117
    Coffee-Toffee Dessert, 118
    Cranberry Ice, 118
    Sorbet, Fresh Orange, 118
  Fruit, Spiced Winter, 25
  Mandelbrot, Star of David, 17
  Soufflés, French Silk, 14

Tiramisù, 115
Trifle, Creamy Citrus, 113
Doughnuts, Spiced Baked, 54
Dressings. *See also* Salad Dressings, Stuffings.
  Bread Dressing, Fruit and Cheese, 95
  Cornbread Dressing, 96

Fat, Figuring the, 9
Fat Limits, Daily, 9
Fettuccine, Crawfish, 81
Filling, Maple-Oat Bread with Prune, 62
Fish. *See also* Crab, Lobster, Shrimp.
  Crawfish Fettuccine, 81
  Swordfish with Citrus-Walnut Sauce, Spicy
    Crusted, 83
Florentine, Crab Quiche, 25
Frankfurter Brenten, 138
Freezing
  Desserts, freezing, 113
  Facts on Freezing, 8
  From Freezer to Table, 8
Frittata, Christmas, 21
Frosting, Cream Cheese, 100
Frosting, Orange Marmalade, 17
Fruit. *See also* specific types.
  Acorn Squash, Fruited, 93
  Beverages
    Mulled Fruit Drink, 38
    Scarlet Sipper, 33
    Spritzer, Citrus, 41
    Tea, Spiced Fruit, 38
    Wine, Hot Mulled, 39
  Cake with Dried Fruit, Holiday, 107
  Compote, Citrus and Dried Fruit, 116
  Compote, Easy Fruit, 23
  Desserts, freezing fruit, 113
  Dip with Almond Chips, Fluffy Fruit, 31
  Dressing, Fruit and Cheese Bread, 95
  Roast, Fruited Cider, 72
  Salad with Fruit, Hearts of Palm, 86
  Spiced Winter Fruit, 25
  Stollen, Dresdner, 65

Garnishing beverages, 38
Gifts
  Bread, Give a Gift of, 59
  Butter, Apple, 124
  Cheese, Potted Herbed, 123
  Chips, Peppered Cheese, 123
  Chutney, Pear and Apple, 125
  Conserve, Cranberry, 125
  Cookies
    Banana Treats, 126
    Bars, Almond Chess, 139
    Biscotti, Hazelnut, 135
    Bizcochitos, 135
    Brownies, Fudgy Chocolate, 139
    Chocolate Icebox Cookies, 130
    Coconut Cookies, Chewy, 126
    Date-Sugar Cookies, 126
    Frankfurter Brenten, 138
    Joulutortut, 137
    Linzer Cookies, 136
    Mint-Chocolate Drops, 128
    Oatmeal-Spice Cookies, 129
    Orange Drops, Frosted, 128
    Peanut Butter Icebox Cookies, 131
    Poppy Seed-Almond Cookies, 129
    Spiced Heart Cookies, 136
    Springerle, 138
    Sugar Cookies, Frosted, 132
    Vanilla Icebox Cookies, 132

Festive Gifts, 137
Gift Giving, 125
Kitchen, Gifts from the, 7
Minicakes, Apple Spice, 140
Mushrooms, Marinated, 122
Mustard, Curried Peppercorn, 123
Peppers, Pickled Sweet, 123
Sauce, Cranberry Jezebel, 124
Snack Mix, Italian Seasoned, 124
Truffles, Mint-Chocolate, 133
Vinegar, Cranberry Wine, 125
Glaze, Fresh Ham with Maple Syrup-Bourbon, 74
Grapefruit-Pecan Bread, 60
Grapefruit Salad with Champagne Dressing, 88
Gravy, Turkey, 97
Greens with Balsamic Vinaigrette, Mixed, 20

Ham
  Dip, Spinach-Ham, 43
  Fresh ham, about, 74
  Fresh Ham with Maple Syrup-Bourbon
    Glaze, 74
  Hopping John, 94
  Quiche, Ham and Cheese, 25
Hazelnut Biscotti, 135
Hearts of Palm Salad with Fruit, 86
Honey-Dijon Pork Tenderloin, 33
Hopping John, 94
Hummus with Pita Wedges, Red Bean, 42

Lamb with Wild Rice-Risotto Stuffing, Crown
  Roast of, 75
Latkes, Potato, 90
Lemon Cream Tart, 110
Lemon-Macaroon Tartlets, 31
Lime Margaritas, Orange-, 41
Linzer Cookies, 136
Lobster with Angel Hair Pasta, Creamy, 83

Macaroon Tartlets, Lemon-, 31
Macaroon Tart Shells, 31
Mandelbrot, 17
Mandelbrot, Star of David, 17
Microwave
  Chicken Bites with Cucumber Dip, Spicy, 46
  Drink, Mulled Fruit, 38
  Freezer to Table, From, 8
  Sweet Potatoes, Cranberry-Glazed, 14
  Truffles, Mint-Chocolate, 133
Muffins
  Cranberry-Citrus Muffins, 56
  Maple-Squash Muffins, 56
  Pear-Walnut Muffins, 57
Mushrooms
  Marinated Mushrooms, 122
  Sauce, Filet Mignon with Mushroom-Wine, 70
  Sauce, Roast Veal with Mushroom, 72
  Turnovers, Curried Mushroom, 30
Mustard, Curried Peppercorn, 123

Oat Bread with Prune Filling, Maple-, 62
Oatmeal-Spice Cookies, 129
Onions
  Dip, Deviled, 29
  Dip, Roasted Sweet Potato, 43
  Potatoes au Gratin, Marsala, 92
  Turkey Cutlets, Holiday, 80
Oranges
  Drops, Frosted Orange, 128
  Frosting, Orange Marmalade, 17

Margaritas, Orange-Lime, 41
Popovers, Orange, 54
Salad, Spinach-Orange, 34
Sorbet, Fresh Orange, 118
Soufflé, Orange Sweet Potato, 92
Trifle, Creamy Citrus, 113
Twist, Orange, 39

P ancakes
Latkes, Potato, 90
Pastas
Angel Hair Pasta, Creamy Lobster with, 83
Fettuccine, Crawfish, 81
Peanut Butter
Cookie Pinwheels, 131
Cookies, Peanut Butter Icebox, 131
Pears
Chutney, Pear and Apple, 125
Coffee Cake, Cardamom, 58
Loaf, Pear and Poppy Seed, 60
Muffins, Pear-Walnut, 57
Tart, Cinnamon-Pear, 20
Peas
Black-Eyed Peas, Spicy, 33
Hopping John, 94
Sugar Snap Peas, Sesame, 90
Pecans
Bread, Grapefruit-Pecan, 60
Cheesecake, Maple-Pecan, 34
Malted Pecans, Brandied Pumpkin-Ice Cream
Pie with, 117
Salad, Wild Rice and Pecan, 88
Tart, Maple-Pecan, 108
Peppers
Chicken Rolls, Italian, 77
Pickled Sweet Peppers, 123
Pizza, Artichoke and Red Pepper, 49
Roasted Pepper Dip, 42
Roasted Peppers, Broccoli with, 13
Pickled Sweet Peppers, 123
Pies and Pastries
Ice Cream Pie with Malted Pecans, Brandied
Pumpkin-, 117
Shells, Macaroon Tart, 31
Turnovers, Curried Mushroom, 30
Pilaf, Barley, Wild Rice, and Currant, 13
Pilaf, Holiday Rice, 93
Pineapple Sauce, 47
Pizza, Artichoke and Red Pepper, 49
Planning holiday meals, 6
Pork
Roasting Tips, 72
Roast Pork with Apricot-Prune Stuffing, 73
Tenderloin, Honey-Dijon Pork, 33
Potatoes. See also Sweet Potatoes.
au Gratin, Marsala Potatoes, 92
Latkes, Potato, 90
Prunes
Filling, Maple-Oat Bread with Prune, 62
Joulutortut, 137
Stuffing, Roast Pork with Apricot-Prune, 73
Pudding, Bittersweet Chocolate, 112
Pudding, Black Bottom Cranberry, 113
Pumpkin
Cake, Pumpkin-Spice Bundt, 104
Ice Cream Pie with Malted Pecans, Brandied
Pumpkin-, 117
Tart, Pumpkin Crème Brûlée, 111

Q uesadillas, Santa Fe Chicken, 47
Quiche Florentine, Crab, 25
Quiche, Ham and Cheese, 25

R agoût of Veal, 19
Raisin Bread, Cinnamon-, 66
Raspberry Spritzers, Cranberry-, 26
Rice
Cornish Hens, Grecian, 77
Hopping John, 94
Pilaf, Barley, Wild Rice, and Currant, 13
Pilaf, Holiday Rice, 93
Wild Rice and Pecan Salad, 88
Wild Rice-Risotto Stuffing, Crown Roast of
Lamb with, 75
Roasting Tips, 72
Rolls, Apple-Filled Sweet, 67
Rolls, Cornmeal Crescent, 34

S alad Dressings
Champagne Dressing, Grapefruit Salad with, 88
Vinaigrette, Mixed Greens with Balsamic, 20
Yogurt-Poppy Seed Dressing, 34
Salads
Cranberry-Applesauce Salad, Layered, 86
Grapefruit Salad with Champagne Dressing, 88
Greens with Balsamic Vinaigrette, Mixed, 20
Hearts of Palm Salad with Fruit, 86
Spinach-Orange Salad, 34
Wild Rice and Pecan Salad, 88
Sauces
Citrus-Walnut Sauce, Spicy Crusted Swordfish
with, 83
Cranberry Jezebel Sauce, 124
Gift Giving, 125
Mushroom Sauce, Roast Veal with, 72
Mushroom-Wine Sauce, Filet Mignon with, 70
Pineapple Sauce, 47
Scones, Cranberry, 23
Scones, Date and Maple, 53
Seafood. See Crab, Fish, Lobster, Shrimp.
Sesame Broccoli, 89
Sesame Sugar Snap Peas, 90
Shrimp
Buffalo Shrimp with Blue Cheese Dip, 29
Creole, Spicy Shrimp, 82
Spread, Shrimp-Chutney, 44
Vinaigrette, Shrimp with Silken Tomato, 48
Snack Mix, Italian Seasoned, 124
Sorbet, Fresh Orange, 118
Soufflés
Cake, Dark Chocolate Soufflé, 100
French Silk Soufflés, 14
Sweet Potato Soufflé, Orange, 92
Sourdough
Bread, Sourdough, 64
Starter Food, 64
Starter, Sourdough, 64
Spinach
Dip, Spinach-Ham, 43
Florentine, Crab Quiche, 25
Salad, Spinach-Orange, 34
Spread, Shrimp-Chutney, 44
Springerle, 138
Squash. See also Zucchini.
Acorn Squash, Fruited, 93
Muffins, Maple-Squash, 56

Stuffings. See also Dressings.
Apricot-Prune Stuffing, Roast Pork with, 73
Bread Stuffing, New England, 95
Wild Rice-Risotto Stuffing, Crown Roast of
Lamb with, 75
Sweet Potatoes
Cakes, Sweet Potato, 16
Dip, Roasted Sweet Potato, 43
Glazed Sweet Potatoes, Cranberry-, 14
Soufflé, Orange Sweet Potato, 92

T arts
Cinnamon-Pear Tart, 20
Crab-Artichoke Tarts, 48
Cream Cheese-Cranberry Tart, 110
Double-Chocolate Cream Tart, 108
Lemon Cream Tart, 110
Lemon-Macaroon Tartlets, 31
Maple-Pecan Tart, 108
Pumpkin Crème Brûlée Tart, 111
Shells, Macaroon Tart, 31
Teriyaki Chicken Drummettes with Pineapple
Sauce, 47
Tiramisù, 115
Tomato Pâté, Smoked Turkey and Sun-Dried, 45
Tomato Vinaigrette, Shrimp with Silken, 48
Tortillas
Chips, Peppered Cheese, 123
Quesadillas, Santa Fe Chicken, 47
Trifle, Creamy Citrus, 113
Truffles, Mint-Chocolate, 133
Turkey
Ballottine, Curried Turkey, 78
Cutlets, Holiday Turkey, 80
Degrease Turkey Drippings, How to, 97
Gravy, Turkey, 97
Pâté, Smoked Turkey and Sun-Dried
Tomato, 45
Roasted Turkey, Herb-, 12
Smoked Turkey, Cranberry Biscuits with, 30

V anilla Icebox Cookies, 132
Veal
Ragoût of Veal, 19
Roasting Tips, 72
Roast Veal with Mushroom Sauce, 72
Vegetables. See also specific types.
Brisket with Vegetables, 71
Chicken, Grandma's Simple Roast, 16
Frittata, Christmas, 21
Rice Pilaf, Holiday, 93
Shrimp Creole, Spicy, 82
Turkey Ballottine, Curried, 78
Vinegars
Cranberry Wine Vinegar, 125
Gift Giving, 125

W alnut Muffins, Pear-, 57
Walnut Sauce, Spicy Crusted Swordfish with
Citrus, 83

Y ogurt-Poppy Seed Dressing, 34

Z ucchini-Streusel Bundt Cake, 105

METRIC EQUIVALENTS

Metric Equivalents for Different Types of Ingredients

A standard cup measure of a dry or solid ingredient will vary in weight depending on the type of ingredient. A standard cup of liquid is the same volume for any type of liquid. Use the following chart when converting standard cup measures to grams (weight) or milliliters (volume).

Standard Cup	Fine Powder (ex. flour)	Grain (ex. rice)	Granular (ex. sugar)	Liquid Solids (ex. butter)	Liquid (ex. milk)
1	140 g	150 g	190 g	200 g	240 ml
¾	105 g	113 g	143 g	150 g	180 ml
⅔	93 g	100 g	125 g	133 g	160 ml
½	70 g	75 g	95 g	100 g	120 ml
⅓	47 g	50 g	63 g	67 g	80 ml
¼	35 g	38 g	48 g	50 g	60 ml
⅛	18 g	19 g	24 g	25 g	30 ml

Useful Equivalents for Liquid Ingredients by Volume

¼ tsp					=	1 ml	
½ tsp					=	2 ml	
1 tsp					=	5 ml	
3 tsp	=	1 tbls		=	½ fl oz	=	15 ml
		2 tbls	= ⅛ cup	=	1 fl oz	=	30 ml
		4 tbls	= ¼ cup	=	2 fl oz	=	60 ml
		5⅓ tbls	= ⅓ cup	=	3 fl oz	=	80 ml
		8 tbls	= ½ cup	=	4 fl oz	=	120 ml
		10⅔ tbls	= ⅔ cup	=	5 fl oz	=	160 ml
		12 tbls	= ¾ cup	=	6 fl oz	=	180 ml
		16 tbls	= 1 cup	=	8 fl oz	=	240 ml
		1 pt	= 2 cups	=	16 fl oz	=	480 ml
		1 qt	= 4 cups	=	32 fl oz	=	960 ml
					33 fl oz	= 1000 ml	= 1 l

Useful Equivalents for Dry Ingredients by Weight

(To convert ounces to grams, multiply the number of ounces by 30.)

1 oz	=	1/16 lb	=	30 g
4 oz	=	¼ lb	=	120 g
8 oz	=	½ lb	=	240 g
12 oz	=	¾ lb	=	360 g
16 oz	=	1 lb	=	480 g

Useful Equivalents for Cooking/Oven Temperatures

	Fahrenheit	Celcius	Gas Mark
Freeze Water	32° F	0° C	
Room Temperature	68° F	20° C	
Boil Water	212° F	100° C	
Bake	325° F	160° C	3
	350° F	180° C	4
	375° F	190° C	5
	400° F	200° C	6
	425° F	220° C	7
	450° F	230° C	8
Broil			Grill

Useful Equivalents for Length

(To convert inches to centimeters, multiply the number of inches by 2.5.)

1 in				=	2.5 cm		
6 in	=	½ ft		=	15 cm		
12 in	=	1 ft		=	30 cm		
36 in	=	3 ft	= 1 yd	=	90 cm		
40 in				=	100 cm	=	1 m